IN VINCULIS, OR

THE PRISONER OF WAR

IN VINCULIS;

OR,

THE PRISONER OF WAR.

BEING,

THE EXPERIENCE OF A REBEL IN TWO FEDERAL
PENS, INTERSPERSED WITH REMINISCENCES
OF THE LATE WAR; ANECDOTES OF
SOUTHERN GENERALS, ETC.

BY A VIRGINIA CONFEDERATE.

PETERSBURG, VA.:
"DAILY INDEX" OFFICE.
1866.

IN VINCULIS OR;
THE PRISONER OF WAR

By A Virginia Confederate

As Published in 1866

Trade Paperback ISBN: 1-58218-323-6
Hardcover ISBN: 1-58218-324-4
eBook ISBN: 1-58218-322-8

Digital Scanning and Publishing is a leader in the electronic republication of historical books and documents. We publish many of our titles as eBooks, as well as traditional hardcover and trade paper editions. DSI is committed to bringing many traditional and little known books back to life, retaining the look and feel of the original work.

©2001 DSI Digital Reproduction
First DSI Printing: May 2001

Published by DIGITAL SCANNING, INC.
Scituate, MA 02066
Toll free: 888-349-4443
Outside U.S. 781-545-2100

www.digitalscanning.com

IN

MEMORY OF

THE GOOD CITIZENS AND GALLANT GENTLEMEN,

WHO GAVE UP THEIR LIVES

IN DEFENCE OF THEIR FAMILIES AND FRIENDS,

IN FRONT OF PETERSBURG,

JUNE 9TH, 1864.

This volume

IS REVERENTLY DEDICATED.

EXPLANO-PREFATORY.

———•———

"ON the 10th of June, General Butler sent a force of infantry under General Gillmore, and cavalry under General Kautz, to capture Petersburg, if possible, and destroy the railroad and common bridges across the Appomattox. The cavalry carried the works on the south side, and penetrated well in towards the town, but were forced to retire. General Gillmore finding the works which he approached very strong, and deeming an assault impracticable, returned to Bermuda Hundreds without attempting one."—*Report of Lieut.-Gen. Grant,* 1864–5.

This is all that General Grant has to say as to his complicity in the wickedness of acquainting me experimentally with the internal arrangements of Federal prisons, and as to his indirect responsibility for this pamphlet; and the trifling importance he attaches to the matter is very conclusively exhibited in the fact that he mistakes the date: it was the *ninth* of June, not the *tenth*.

Of this *fiasco* of the immortal enemy of secession-
ists and spoons, I was for five months an unhappy
victim. What I saw, and heard, and did during that
period, I have endeavored, in plain phrase and unem-
bellished, to detail in the following pages. They
were originally written in Richmond, in the winter
of 1864–5, and "set up" as fast as written, so that
by dint of much exertion I managed to get an edition
printed, and about a third of it sold, before a very
melancholy morning in April, when, after seeing
Breckenridge dash over the burning bridge near
which he had sat on his horse for an hour (to be
sure there was nothing more to be done in Richmond), I turned into Main-street to find a squad of
Federal cavalry galloping into town, elate with the
honor of running up the stars and stripes over our
placid old capitol. But alas and alack! before midday I saw the store which contained my unsold
copies bow its head to the blast of that terrible conflagration which yet scars—and for many a day will
scar—our beautiful city.

The winter has come again, and I have thought
that these long, cosy evenings, which not all the
weakness and wickedness of man can take from us,
might be agreeably passed in running over the pages
of a copy of my little narrative, and refitting it for
publication. One reason more than all others moves
me to this conclusion.

Through books, newspapers, magazines, military commissions, congressional legislation, proclamations, reports, novels, "so called," and histories that are far more romantic, the North is not only writing the story of the late war, but the *character* of their late enemies. A great deal of this, from proclamations up, *we* know to be false, but the time has not come, nor does every one who feels the need feel the power to do justice. Each Southern man, though, may and ought to contribute something to our own story of this war, even though it be as pure a trifle as this. The living claim it, and the inexpressibly loved and honored dead demand it. And I hope to live to see the day when the infamous atrocities of Hunter, in the Valley of Virginia, will have a fitting historian; when the monstrous tyranny and knavery of New Orleans rule will be exposed; when the secrets of the Bastiles will be given up; when the murders of Missouri and Tennessee shall be heralded to the world; and, above all, when the story of that hellish carnival of lust, and rapine, and outrage, and arson, and murder, and nameless villanies which Yankee poets and magazine writers euphoniously name the "Great March from the Mountains to the Sea," shall be painted with a broad brush and a free hand, that mankind may shudder again to think of the crimes committed in the name of LIBERTY!

It has been objected that no good can come of such

disclosures—that nothing but reproach to the American name can follow them—that such recriminations can only postpone the day of peace.

I answer, that the Southern people can be expected to have little interest in the American name, while they are denied American privileges, and we shall very contentedly see the American name suffer any reproach that truth can bring upon it. Nor do I think that while Jefferson Davis and C. C. Clay, and their compatriots, are denounced in official proclamations as *assassins,* the people of the United States can close the mouth of any accuser who offers reproach to the American name.

As to *the day of peace,* there are many people in the South whose faith is so weak, that in despair of the enjoyment of that blessing they have turned their thoughts to the nearer probability of the millennium.

The reader's pardon, a thousand times—I grow political; and *in a Preface!*—fy!

I conclude by saying that I had the good fortune to be confined in the best two of the Federal pens, according to the unanimous statement of experts in the matter of imprisonment, and that I shall have, therefore, fewer stories to tell of those systematic hardships which wear away the lives and spirits of men, than many hundreds and thousands of my fellow Confederates (who survive their jails and jailers) might write.

What I have written, however, is the mere amplification of a diary which I kept throughout my prison-life, and which, on starting homeward, I sewed up in my clothing, to my great fear and perpetual bodily discomfort for many days.

I cannot lay down my pen without expressing the hope that the day of the end of persecution and pro-scription may not be put off, as many seem desirous of postponing it, till the present generation passes away.

It is puerile to invoke, at this day, the mantle of oblivion for the crimes of this war on either side; and since the facts must be known, it is well that *all* should be known, not only that no injustice be done by the partial historian, but that generations to come may be warned to try every peaceful remedy for intolerable evils, much more for those which are endurable, before they plunge themselves into that epitome of all human crimes and mortal woes which men call War.

CONTENTS.

CHAPTER I.

Absit omen.—Cavalry advancing.—To the front.—Choice of weapons.—Company E, Twelfth Virginia Infantry, A. N. V.   13

CHAPTER II.

The battle opens.—The first charge repulsed.—Artillery coming to help us.—Overpowered.—A prisoner   20

CHAPTER III.

The advance checked.—Gilmore fails.—Marching off.—An escape.—At Kautz's quarters.—First prison feed.—An interview with the general.—Transferred   27

CHAPTER IV.

Beast Butler   36

CHAPTER V.

To Bermuda Hundreds.—Black guard.—Awful swearing.—A cold night.—Down the river.—Prison thieves.—Andersonville and Wirz.—Leaving Fortress Monroe.—Maryland   46

CHAPTER VI.

Point Lookout.—A brute.—The Pen.—Lyon's Den.—A friend in need.—The demoralization of prison-life 56

CHAPTER VII.

Order of exorcises.—Fabrications of the Sanitary Commission.— History of the pen.—Official clothes thieves.—The guards.— Black guards again 64

CHAPTER VIII.

Shelter at Point Lookout.—Cracker-box houses.—A prison adventure.—Prison ingenuity.—The washerwomen.—Contributions to prisoners.—The war a people's war.—A woman.—A loyal negro 71

CHAPTER IX.

Black patriots on the rampage.—Major Weymouth's inspection.— Foul water.—Columbia.—Rumored capture of Petersburg.— Peculiar costume.—The rationale of rations 84

CHAPTER X.

Officers moving.—Negro insolence.—Fires out across the dead line.—Improvising furniture.—Designs on a "nail kag."— Negro regiment to the front.—A new prison at Elmira.—The Fourth of July *in vinculis.*—Noble Maryland 96

CHAPTER XI.

More arrivals.—The sinking of the Alabama.—"Miss Gilbert's Career."—Old Jubal after the Suabians.—A disagreeable order.—Working details.—Changing quarters 108

CHAPTER XII.

Deliverance against sea-going.—A disgusting trip.—A Good Samaritan.—Nectar.—New York harbor.—On the Erie Railroad.—Sympathizers.—At Elmira.—El Cid anathematized   117

CHAPTER XIII.

Statistics of Elmira Pen.—The officers.—Samples of Federal cruelty.—Number of prisoners.—Barrack accommodations   128

CHAPTER XIV.

Matters medical.—Sanger the sanguinary.—Rebel doctors.—Cruel neglect of the sick.—Deaths at Elmira and Andersonville contrasted.—The Commissary Department.—Punishments   138

CHAPTER XV.

De minimis.—Withstanding temptation.—The author seeking office—And getting it   148

CHAPTER XVI.

Arcadian experience.—A terrible accident.—Neglect of the victims.—A note from Madam Ik Marvel.—An observatory.—Loyalty and sight-seeing.—Preaching in camp.—The campaign in a diagram.—A reminiscence of Jeb Stuart.—The negroes on guard.—Petersburg in flames.—Heavy eating.—Chess   154

CHAPTER XVII.

Sermons.—A political bloodhound of Zion.—Clothing proscribed.—Disgusting obscenity.—The Tallahassee.—A comrade dies.—A contraband.—More restrictive orders.—A sharp retort.—Scurvy.—A note by "underground."—Awful mortality.—Digging out.—Pursuit fruitless   166

CHAPTER XVIII.

Exchange rumors.—A subterfuge.—Unfit for duty for sixty
days.—Apply for a nurse's post.—Rebel no reproach.—Tricks
to obtain an exchange.—Paroling the sick.—Off for Dixie   178

CHAPTER XIX.

Leaving Elmira.—The trip to Baltimore.—Seven die on the
train.—Arrival in Baltimore.—Benevolent ladies.—A stratagem.—Off for Point Lookout.—Official thieving.—Major
Brady.—Massachusetts in 1775.—Stonewall Jackson.—His last
fight.—A memory.—Stonewall Jackson's way   189

CHAPTER XX.

Pen routine.—Diagnosis.—Plundering the prisoners.—Off for
Dixie.—The Northern Light.—The Merrimac and Commodore
Vanderbilt.—Hampton Roads.—Mitchelltown.—Servus servo-
rum.—A strange history.—Savannah.—Home!   203

IN VINCULIS;

OR,

THE PRISONER OF WAR.

---◆◆◆---

CHAPTER I.

Absit omen.—Cavalry advancing.—To the front.—Choice of weapons.—Company E, Twelfth Virginia Infantry, A. N. V.

In the blessed days of the troubadours, no contest, personal or political, was deemed lawfully begun unless some stalwart stentor, yclept a herald, chosen, if I rightly remember my Froissart, with a double reference to his strength of lung and proficiency in lying, made a preliminary flourish to prepare the world for the performances about to ensue.

Very much after this fashion it is religiously believed by young ladies who swear by L. E. L., and are neglectful of tucking combs, that the fates, in advance of every important event of our lives, provide, mercifully, some premonitory omens of the ap proaching stroke, that no man may lawfully challenge his doom by exclaiming with university dunces, "Not prepared, sir."

There never was a more groundless fallacy in the

long list of errors of opinion, chargeable to these dear victims of dyspepsia and dactyls.

Dame Fortune commences hostilities in ninety per cent. of her wars without blowing a trumpet, launching a proclamation, or firing the mildest of blank cartridges across our doomed bows, quietly ambushing the best of us in the most flowery valleys, buffeting and persecuting us to the top of her bothersome bent, without so much as, "By your leave, sir."

Small marvel then that the 9th day of June, 1864, dawned—I suppose it did, but never can swear of my own knowledge to *dawns*—with as fair a face upon me, and as bright a promise as the best of her lovely sisters in all that queenly spring.

No croaking crow cawed unusual presages of evil to our quiet little city; no friendly geese cackled their *"qui v'là?"* to intruding barbarians, winning the immortal gratitude of modern Quirites: there were no portents in earth or air; and though on the day in question, I, and many a better man, came to exceeding grief, I had not the remotest cause to apprehend that I should fail that day to relish my two meals (the third long since sacrificed to patriotism), in intramural comfort, and "turn in" at night to as sound a sleep as though I was not compassing the destruction of "the best government the world ever saw." Heaven forgive me.

     *   *   *   *   *   *   *   *

I was sitting in my office peacefully engaged in endeavoring to extract from the Richmond papers, just received, something like an idea of "the situation," when, as though our city were blessed with a patent fire-telegraph, all the available bell-metal in the corporation broke into chorus with so vigorous a peal, and a clangor so resonant, as to suggest to the uninitiated a general conflagration. Not being connected with the fire-brigade, and being otherwise totally disinterested on the subject of inflammable real estate, I might have remained absorbed in my inquiries, and thus escaped my fate (and you these pages), but for the general understanding, if not order, that this signal, theretofore consecrated to the annunciation of fire, should thenceforth in Petersburg serve the purpose, further, of heralding the approach of another "devouring element,"—the Yankees. Thus it came to pass, that in most indecent haste I let fall my journals and hastened into the street, to learn from the first excited passer-by that the enemy's cavalry to the number of twenty thousand—so ran the tale—were approaching the city, and already within two miles of where my informant stood! The "usual discount" of seventy-five per cent. still left the tale uncomfortable to a degree.

"What forces have we on the Jerusalem plank-road (the road by which they were approaching), do you know?"

"Not a d—n man (we had not had—I remark parenthetically—a revival of religion in our town for some time, and Confederate whisky would make a nun swear) except Archer's Battalion, and not a hundred and fifty of them."

Archer's Battalion was an organization of militiamen armed for local defence, and formed of the non-conscribable population. It was, therefore, composed of citizens least fitted for military service, but in preparation for the gigantic struggle which, General Lee foresaw, the vast Federal superiority of numbers would impose on him, he could spare no young arm well from his ranks.

Here was what the gentlemen of the P. R. would call "another bloody go."

Military criticism was, however, obviously out of place just then, though, like all my fellow Americans, I affirm my competence, and claim my right to hold forth on that theme as the spirit moves, so I turned the key in my office door—destined, alas! to remain untouched by hand of mine for many a moon—and calling by my home to replenish my commissariat, I sallied forth prepared (morally speaking let it be understood) to do battle *à l'outrance,* against all comers of the Yankee persuasion, though they had been as numerous as Abe's jokes, Ben. Butler's thieveries, or the leaves in that umbrageous Spanish valley which has done such incalculable service to simile-mongers since the days of our greatest great-grandmothers.

Admonished by the example of Tristam Shandy, whose amiable desire to acquaint his friends and the world with every thing possible to be known of himself, leads him into most indecorous developments in the first three chapters of his autobiography, I shall not undertake to explain, but only state the fact that I was at that time not in "active service" in any capacity—though it is due to my family, to say that I was *not* in the Nitre and Mining Bureau, a member of the society of Friends, nor the editor of a newspaper. One result of this unattached condition was, that like "Black Dan" in the halcyon days after Tippecanoe was *translated,* I was somewhat puzzled to know "whither I should go." Another difficulty was, the vagueness of my idea what to do when I got there; but as the place to be useful was obviously the line of the enemy's approach, I turned my face thither and soon found myself in the camp of Major Archer's Battalion, where all was preparation. This was about two miles from the city, or a mile southeast of the Blandford Cemetery, and exactly at the point known in the subsequent operations around Petersburg as Rives' House—not very far from "The Mine."

I found here a very stimulating degree of excitement. The battalion understanding perfectly well that a fight at very great odds was before it, and being so small that the accession of a single volunteer was not to be slighted, was marching by companies to assigned positions in the little earthwork before its tents; and breathless couriers, racing at the highest speed possible to Confederate steeds, were momently arriving with news of the leisurely advance of General Kautz.

Reporting to the first captain I met, he made the obvious suggestion that I should get a musket; and I hastened to the ordnance officer to supply myself. This gentleman courteously invited me to make intelligent choice between three specimens of smoothbore military architecture, universally known in the army as "altered percussions"—guns originally with flint locks, and therefore demonstrably a quarter of a century old, but modernized by the substitution of the percussion hammer and tube. These hybrids, without bayonets, were the weapons with which that handful of militia were to resist (or fly before) the picked cavalry (and many regiments of them) of the Yankee army.

One of these formidable arquebuses had a trigger with so weak a spring that the tenderest cap ever turned out of a laboratory would successfully resist its pressure; the second was so rusty that its ramrod shrank from sounding its oxydized depths; while the third, which had the "spit and span" appearance of an assistant surgeon or a regimental adjutant on dress parade, proved on examination to be so bent and wrenched that you could not see light through it when the breech-pin was unscrewed! I now began to be overwhelmed with apprehensions that I was destined to act exclusively as a lay figure in the drama about to be put on the boards, and my vanity not a little recoiled from the prospect of playing dummy in the game, when a friend, commiserating my perplexity, handed me a gun left in his tent by a comrade who had gone to town "on leave" that morning, and who was not likely to return. I soon balanced the "provant" which filled one of my pockets with ammunition enough to fill the other; and accounting myself "armed and equipped as the law directs," I stepped forward to the earthwork.

Several months had elapsed since I quit soldiering proper, leaving behind me at Orange Courthouse the noblest company of gentlemen that ever perilled their lives as private soldiers in any cause or country; and I longed for them that day, with the immortal "Twelfth Virginia," in which they marched, that they might stand by their sires at the portal of their home, and "keep the gate."

Glorious boys! There is not an acre in the long line of the circumvallation of Petersburg that is not vocal with some gallant deed of their achieving; and when the death-struggle came they abandoned their city, not their cause, fought their weary way to Appomattox Courthouse, dealt the last successful blows at the foe, and ere they stacked arms for the last time divided among them the tatters of their untarnished flag, that memory might never want a souvenir of a career glorious and unsullied from its first hour to its last.

The fairy days are passed, and my comrades came not for my wishing; and I who had been proud to stand amid the sons, was content to stand that day amid their sires. *Sang azul* I suspect, for, as that morning's work showed, as stout hearts beat beneath gray locks as beneath gray jackets.

CHAPTER II.

The battle opens.—The first charge repulsed.—Artillery coming to
help us.—Overpowered.—A prisoner.

THE sun was clambering up the sky—a figure which
astronomy has perpetually but vainly tilted against
since the great Italian's day—and the town-clock had
struck ten, many minutes before, when a pair of frantio
videttes—one of them without his hat—tore into
camp on foaming steeds, with the news that the
enemy, not more than a half a mile away, were rapid
ly approaching in a body consisting of several regiments of cavalry, and at least four pieces of artillery.
Our "position" was an open earthwork—the front
face of which was cut at right angles by the Jerusalem
plankroad—a thoroughfare which, some outside barbarians may not know, opens up to deserving Petersburgers, in times of peace, the beatific vision of Sussex
hams and Southampton brandy. This work, intended
to accommodate two pieces of artillery, but then all
innocent of ordnance, was accompanied by a line of
low breastworks running out on either flank to afford
shelter to such infantry as might be destined to support the guns, while beyond, on each side, lay a level
and accessible country, inviting easy approach to man
or beast. There was nothing in the character of the

position to give the assailed any advantage other than that which the breastwork offered in case of a direct attack the ground being almost a dead level in every direction, and when Major Archer, our commandant, disposed his little force of about one hundred and twenty-five men along the extended line—six hundred yards, I presume—it was perfectly evident that twenty thousand cavalry, or any respectable minority of the same, would make short work of us. In conformity to universal civilized precedent, the major addressed us a word of cheer and counsel before he assigned us our position; but there was eloquence incomparably superior to all the witchery of words in the hundred homes which stood but a scant cannon-shot behind us, and in the reflection that, according as we did our devoir, there might be, then and thenceforth, grief or rejoicing to them and to many more. Small marvel then, that as I looked down our little band, sparsely stretched over our extended and exposed front, and noticed how well the best of my townsmen were represented in its ranks, I felt that they would give an account of themselves that no wife or mother, sweetheart or sister, would blush to hear or remember, though every Cossack that ever swam the Don should charge our line that day—an account that the brave boys keeping watch and ward before Grant's legions would toss their tattered caps in air to hear.

We expended a few moments in closing our lines at the point at which the road cut them, with an old wagon and a score or two of fence-rails disposed *à la chevaux de frise*, and *waited*.

We had not long to wait: a cloud of dust in our front, told of the hurried advance of cavalry, and the next instant, the glitter of spur and scabbard revealed to us a long line of horsemen, rapidly deploying under cover of a wood that ran parallel to our line, and about half a mile in front of us. *Then we missed our cannon:* our venerable muskets were not worth a tinker's imprecation at longer range than a hundred yards, and we were compelled, *per force,* to watch the preparations for our capture or slaughter, much after the fashion that a rational turtle may be presumed to contemplate the preliminaries of a civic dinner in London. A little of that military coquetry called re-connoissance, determined our enemy to feel us first with a small portion of his command, and on came, at a sweeping gallop, a gallant company of troopers with as confident an air as though all that was necessary was that they should "come" and "see" in order to "conquer." Every one saw that this was a party we could easily manage, and we possessed, therefore, our souls in great patience, till we could see the chevrons on the arm of the non-commissioned officer who led them—a brave fellow—and then there broke forth (from such amiable muskets as could be induced to go off) a discharge that scattered the cavaliers like chaff, —three riderless horses being all of the expedition that entered our lines.

The incident was trifling in the extreme, but it saved Petersburg, and probably prolonged for months the surrender.

The Federals now became convinced that no cav-alry charge would frighten these ununiformed and half-armed militiamen from their posts, and that a regular attack *au pied* must be made. For this purpose two regiments of their cavalry were dismounted and deployed on either side of the road, in a line double the length of our own, and it was evident that they had determined to flank us on both sides.

The welcome rattle of artillery horses brought now a cheer to every lip as we observed two field-pieces falling into position on our right, and the sharp shriek of a shell curvetting over the Yankee line, was an agreeable variation of the monotonous silence in which, to the right and left, their skirmish line was stretching away to encompass us. This occasioned another check, and provoked an artillery response, which continued for twenty minutes, with about the effect currently attributed to sacred melodies chanted in the hearing of a certain useful hybrid, deceased. But these were all golden moments for Petersburg— cannon and horses were pouring into town. Graham's and Sturdivant's batteries were wheeling into position, and Dearing was hastening to the scene with his cavalry,—Dearing, the gallant trooper, who gave away his noble life in the gathering gloom of the last hours of the Confederacy. "Green be the turf above thee!"

Meanwhile, the long line of foemen was stretching around us—manifold more than we in numbers, and, as we soon found, armed with the Spencer rifle, repeating sixteen times. And there we fought them; fought them till we were so surrounded, that the two nearest men to me were shot *in the back* while facing the line of original approach; till both our guns were captured; till our camp, in rear of the works, was

full of the foe; till the noblest blood of our city
stained the clay of the breastwork as they gave out
their lives, gun in hand and face foeward, on the spot
where their officers placed them. Their faces rise
before me now, the calm grave countenances of Ban-
nister and Staubley; the generous, joyous frankness of
Friend and Hardy; the manly, conscientious fire of
patriotism in all—Bellingham and Blanks, Jones,
Johnson, and the rest—all gallant gentlemen and
true; one of whose lives was well worth a heca-
tomb of the bummers and bounty-jumpers before
them; and I could but ask myself then as now, the
prophetic question whose answer has in all ages sustained the martyrs of freedom as of faith, *"Can such
blood fall in vain?"*

Truly, the cause is lost, but no man, in all the ages,
died for what he thought the right and true, in absolute fruitlessness.

One by one, my comrades of an hour fell around me
—Bellingham, the last: and as I turned, at his request,
and stooped, to change his position to one of greater
comfort, the enemy trooped over the earthwork behind
me, and the foremost, presenting his loaded carbine,
demanded my surrender with an unrepeatable violence
of language that suggested bloodshed. All avenue of
escape being cut off, I yielded with what grace I could
to my fate, captive to the bow and spear of a hatchet-
fuced member of the First District Cavalry, greatly
enamored of this honorable opportunity of going to
the rear.

He conveyed me to Major Wetherell, the provost-
marshal of General Kautz's command, who was gath-

ering the animate and inanimate spoils of the day—
the latter consisting of our muskets, all of which, with
utter disregard for their age and manifest infirmities,
he incontinently smashed. At this point I had the
satisfaction of seeing a Yank, whose haste to destroy
our guns was so great, that he would not take time to
withdraw the load, blow a very ugly hole in his thigh
—an accident whereon his Yankeeship is probably
moralizing to this hour.

The cavalry, who had not dismounted, now swept
by us towards the city, whose spires were in full view,
in confident expectation of an easy capture, and as
soon as they passed, the prisoners were brought together to be enrolled.

An inexcusable weakness for looking at the droll
side of every thing overcame, for a moment, my apprehensions for the safety of the city, and my sorrow
and shock over the loss of my friends; though the latter sentiment, has, alas! received rude treatment
many a time and oft during this bloody war.

And indeed a graver personage might have been
pardoned a smile, for a more varied collection of
heroes never blessed the eyes of man in the same
compass, I suspect.

Several of my comrades were many years over fifty,
while some had not passed their second decade, and
their pursuits were as diverse as their ages. Although so few in number, I noticed among my fellow-
captives, tradesmen and farmers, clerks and school-
masters, merchants and millers, manufacturers and
magistrates, the city chamberlain, a member of the
legislature, and a chaplain! In the matter of uniform

2

and soldierly appearance, we were as motley a crew as the memorable squad of recruits that Sir John swore he would not lead through Coventry.

Among the prisoners were two old gentlemen who had been taken up while attending to the business of their farms; not only non-combatants, but in the case of one of them, a man so deaf that he had heard no voice that was not a shout for a dozen years. Yet his generous captors refused him permission (the only favor he asked) to go to his home, which was not a hundred yards off, and see that his children (all girls) were safe from the bullets and the brutes that were sometimes found in conjunction in the Federal armies.

He was silenced while appealing for the poor boon with a threat against his life and a volley of oaths, and was subsequently hurried off to prison with the rest of us, where he contracted a fever which broke a hearty constitution, and ultimately hastened, if it did not cause his death.

When I add that he was perhaps the most uncompromising Union man in Eastern Virginia in the great struggle of 1860, no one within her limits will fail to recall that generous friend, that sterling patriot, and that honest man, Hon. Timothy Rives, of Prince George, the war-horse of Democracy.

In the fall of '65, we buried him in the midst of the desolation with which war had scourged his happy home, within sight of the spot where he had such an vain for permission to give a farewell and a blessing to his motherless daughters.

CHAPTER III.

The advance checked.—Gilmore fails.—Marching off.—An escape.—
At Kautz's quarters.—First prison feed.—An interview with the
general.—Transferred.

A LIEUTENANT was busily engaged in recording
our names and companies—here I was forced to im-
provise, as I did not know the letter of mine—and we
were conjuring up sad images of the sack of our city
by the profane devils around us—and who ever heard
such profanity as the Federal army was filled with?—
when a shell came booming over us with a welcome
whistle, for it betokened resistance at a point where
we thought our city defenceless. Another and another! and emerging from the lane down which, a
few moments before, they had turned with such evident anticipation of easy conquest, we saw the rear,
now by a "bout face" the front, of the Yankee column retreating with Gilpin speed.

The propriety of postponing all formalities respecting the prisoners became now quite evident, and,
under a heavy escort, we were ordered back to camp.

A direct route to the pontoon bridge which Butler
the Eminent had stretched across the Appomattox
at Point of Rocks, and which we would have to cross,
would have required perhaps ten miles of travel. As
it was, we marched twenty-six.

General Gilmore, who had been intrusted with the

infantry attack, had failed, and it was thought pru-
dent, therefore, to follow the apostolic example and
"fetch a compass." I think we "boxed" it.

Jaded with the fatigue, excitement, and exposure
of the fight, and urged at the sabre point by the cavalry, who, whether through spleen or fear, seemed
bent on driving us like cattle, we had a dolorous time
of it, and on arriving within half a mile of the river,
at eleven P. M., a more forlorn set of Confederates
never trusted in "Deo Vindice."*

Once or twice I got a "lift" from some benevolent
trooper, who recognized the difficulty which bipeds
experience in matching the speed of animals of more
liberal ambulatory endowments; and before we had
gone very far, the assistant provost-marshal, Lieutenant
W. E. Bird, introduced himself by an inquiry after his
uncle, a well-known citizen of Petersburg. This introduction was fruitful of certain liquid comforts, to which it
is needless to make more particular allusion; and long
before we arrived at our journey's end we had established a *rapport*—a canteen being the *medium*.

This is a circumstance I mention most unblushingly,
inasmuch as it is my religious conviction that neither
Father Matthew nor John B. Gough would have been
able to stand the temptations, social, mental, moral,
physical, digestive, and patriotic, that lay in wait for
the starving Confederates during the last two years of
their unequal struggle.

---

* There may possibly be some reader who does not know
that this was the motto on the state seal of the Confederacy,
the device of which was a man on horseback, with this legend.

Before crossing the river, we were halted, as I have said, and the roll called, when, to the surprise of some, the provost-marshal's bill of lading did not correspond with the consignment—there was one man missing, the Reverend Mr. Hall, chaplain of the Washington Artillery, that gallant corps of Crescent City gentlemen, who, under Walton, won their spurs at Manassas, and bore their banner bravely under Eshelman to the death.

Mr. Hall had come out to the trenches after the fight began, in order to bring news to a lady in Petersburg, at whose house he was stopping, of the fate of her husband. Though unarmed, a non-combatant, and a mere spectator, he was seized by the Yanks, put into line with the rest, and hurried off despite his protest, and despite the fact that, by solemn agreement, army chaplains had been exempted on both sides from liability to detention as prisoners of war. On the march I was introduced to him—misery acquainting us oftentimes with agreeable as well as *strange* bedfellows, and found that he had serious apprehensions of falling into Butler's hands—a worthy whose tender mercies he had enjoyed in New Orleans, and whose character and acts he had characterized in just, and therefore disagreeable terms, in a publication in the Southern newspapers shortly after the Beast drove him from the city.

Unwilling, therefore, to fall again into that saint's power, he contrived to escape by obtaining permission to ride in an ambulance, which soon got separated from that portion of the column in which the rest of the prisoners were; and when the party stopped he quietly slipped out of the wagon, plunged into the woods, the night being as dark as the population of Mitcheltown, and thus escaped.

The Provost-marshal's wrath was excessive and profane at this *contretemps,* and he endeavored to shield himself from the charge of neglect, by insisting that Mr. Hall had given his parole not to attempt to escape—quite a likely story.

While stopping here, the rest of the discomfited brigade overtook us, and filing by, crossed the pontoon bridge before us. We followed them, entered Chesterfield County, tramping along a well-beaten road lined with tents, and with all the appointments and appearance of a huge camp.

It was past midnight as we neared General Kautz's headquarters, some three miles from Bermuda Hundreds. A filthy log-hut, which was used as a guardhouse, was pointed out to us as our hotel; and footsore, weary, hungry, and blanketless, we threw ourselves on the ground to take our first sleep as captives.

I had hardly disposed myself for a nap when I heard my name called at the door; and on answering, was invited to accept a blanket and a berth in the tent of my canteen acquaintance, Lieutenant Bird. I accepted *nem con.*

Of course, I ought now to have spent at least an hour meditating on the stirring and unusual events of the day, planning measures of escape, congratulating myself on the safety of Petersburg, berating the Yankees, or wafting to the sympathizing stars affectionate messages to—none of your business whom. Alas! with much humiliation do I confess, my hand on my mouth and my face in the dust, not all nor any of these things did I. Doffing my shoes—no old soldier sleeps in his shoes—I stretched myself on the floor, wrapped a blanket around me, and with a "Good-morning, Bird," fell straightway into so profound a sleep, that if eyes soft or stern flashed on me in dreams that night, they left no trace on my waking memory then, nor leave they any now.

It was broad day when I shook myself out of my blanket, at the instance of a friendly-voiced son of Vaterland, who administered a little spirituous consolation, besides furnishing me with a bucket of water and a towel; and in a few moments I was ready for a visit to my comrades, whose complaints of their several discomforts during the night argued a very indifferent appreciation of the lodging accommodations of their quarters.

It was not long before all other sources of complaint vanished before the gnawing claims of vulgar hunger, which, in healthy subjects, gobbles up minor calamities as incontinently as Aaron's rod swallowed the wands of the Copts; and we utterly refused to be comforted, because rations were not.

It was quite nine A. M., when a barrel of "Salt horse" and a couple of boxes of "hard tack" were deposited at the door of our pen, and flanking them, was a keg of most odorous sourrout, and a small supply of potatoes.

Salt horse is *army* for mess beef, as hard tack is for the dry, hard crackers with which armies in motion are generally fed. Potatoes are the inspiration of Irishmen! sourrout is——the devil!

We were dividing out our "provender" with soldierly equity, when, very much to my amazement, an
orderly hallooed at the door that General Kautz
wished to see *me,* and hoping that there might be
some good news for the citizen prisoners, several of
whom were in our party—possibly their release—I
abandoned my rations (an insanity I ought to have
been above falling into), and in a few minutes found
myself in the presence of the celebrated raider.
Kautz is a man of about five feet ten inches in height,
I should suppose, though I only saw him in a sitting
position; has a swarthy complexion, a square massive
German head, wears his hair and beard cut close,
speaks slowly and thoughtfully, and has the breeding
of a gentleman. He desired me to take a seat, offered
a cigar, and we were soon engaged in a free conversation, which was protracted for a couple of hours.

I did not hesitate to tell him how insignificant the
force opposed to him in his attack of the previous day
was, and asked him, with as innocent an expression as
I could assume, why he did not enter Petersburg
after passing us? He very frankly replied:

"Only because I did not know how I could get out
again. The failure of the expedition on the river
roads, which was relied on to support me, made it
necessary to be cautious, and while I might have
dashed into town and burned some property, I might
have lost my command."

In the course of the conversation I learned that he
was a West pointer and the schoolmate of General
Pickett, as well as several other Confederate officers
about whom he inquired. He was, by education, an

infantry man, and observed that he thought the Government had spoiled a good infantry soldier by giving him a cavalry command. I discovered also that the general was somewhat piqued at his failure to receive credit with the Southern people for what he had done. He claimed to have planned and led the expedition that resulted in Morgan's capture on the Ohio the year before, and yet had hardly been mentioned in connection with it. But what surprised him most was, that in the late raid which he had made around the south of Petersburg, his name had escaped notice except in one or two instances, where *it was misspelled,* while the credit or discredit of the expedition was divided between Colonel Spears, who served under him, and General Custer, who was not present.

The alleged superiority of Yankee cavalry seemed to inspire him with great confidence in the early subjugation of the "rebels," and he did not hesitate to express the opinion that the war would be closed by successful raids, and by the greater efficiency and better discipline of that branch of the Federal service. I thought of all this with very unchristian satisfaction some months later, when Hampton entered the Yankee store-room and cut out splendid cattle by the thousand under Kautz's very nose; and again, later still, a week or two, when Hoke captured his last gun, and sent his last squadron flying in irremediable confusion, down the Darbytown road, to the very foot of Birney's infantry.

One thing I found General Kautz fully impressed with and very frank to acknowledge—the splendid fighting qualities of the Southern people. "I may

2*

safely say this," he remarked, in the course of our conversation, "whatever be the issue of this war, we shall have a higher respect for your courage and military skill forever hereafter." He appeared very much annoyed at certain acts of outrage committed by his men in Greensville and Surry, on his last raid, of which he heard the first, as he informed me, from my lips, and deplored the impossibility of preventing such acts, especially among cavalry, where it is so easy to leave and return to the column, and so difficult for officers to prevent misconduct.

He remarked, however, that we in the East had no idea what the depredations and violence of war were. To see and feel these, one must make a cavalry campaign in Tennessee or Missouri. Subsequent events, reaching to this hour, confirm General K.'s observations; for the savageism is producing its bitter harvest of proscription and death to this day in those States, as though the war, in the language of the monster who rules one of them, "had ended two years too soon."

On the whole, I was quite favorably impressed with this officer, and regard my interview with him as among the most pleasant episodes of my sojourn *in Partibus infidelium.*

The arrival of Colonel Spears put an end to our conference, and I returned to my comrades to find the hard-tack dwindling, and potatoes gone, and nothing left of the "krout" but an odor so strong and so diabolical that I am firmly persuaded that he who examines the site of that log-hut a century hence will find that—

    "The scent of the sourkrout will cling to it still."

I had little time to indulge regrets, however; for before many minutes we were ordered to fall in for General Butler's headquarters, and our baggage being as scant as that of the Hibernian, who refused to buy a trunk, because, if he put any thing in it, he would have to go naked, we soon got into line, and a half-hour's march brought us to the headquarters of the Beast—a personage who, on many accounts, deserves a separate chapter.

CHAPTER IV.

Beast Butler.

ON approaching Butler's quarters, which were quite handsomely located, out of reach of all intrusion, the first thing that attracted attention was the presence and prominence of *the negro*. So far we had only seen one or two of the negro soldiers on duty at the pontoon bridge, and the night being as dark as themselves, we could with difficulty distinguish them—but *there* Abyssinia ruled the roast. It was "nigger" everywhere; and although the white soldiers were obviously annoyed at the companionship, the terror of Butler's rule crushed all resistance even of opinion, and the colored brethren knew, and presumed on, their secured position and importance.

We were ranged out in front of His Majesty's tent, and there kept standing hour after hour in one of the hottest suns that I ever felt in any month or at any place. Most of the party were men past middle age, and, with hardly an exception, they had had but one meal, and that a miserable one, for twenty-four hours. When I add that they had fought two hours and marched nearly thirty miles in the same interval, and that a sufficient shade was within a couple of hundred yards of us, it may be easily imagined that our first impressions of "the brute" were not by any means rose-colored.

The afternoon was about half-spent, when an order came for the first three men in line to report to him; and as I chanced to head the list, I heard my name handed in first by his orderly, and was soon summoned into the general's presence. There were two other persons in the tent: one a clerk or amanuensis, who recorded in short-hand the somewhat protracted conversation which subsequently occurred; the other a complacent individual, whose only and obviously agreeable occupation consisted in admiring his new uniform. My eyes were, of course, fixed principally on Butler, and the first and most pervasive thought that crossed my mind was one of profound gratitude to God, who creates no mortal enemy to man without clothing it with features that excite the instant and instinctive aversion of the entire human race. How deadly would the cobra and tarantula be, if Providence had not made them as loathsome as they are venomous! To Benjamin F. Butler's face scarce an element is wanting of absolute repulsiveness. Rapacity finds appropriate expression in his vulture nose—sensuality in his heavy pendant jaws—despotism in his lowering eyebrow; and to these facial charms is added an optical derangement which permits him to scrutinize you with his left eye—the one he seems to place most dependence on—while the right, revolving in a different plane, and concerned, you would imagine, about separate objects—wanders away in another field of vision. Add to this a cool complacency of speech and gesture, which assures you,

that he is on the best of terms with his portly self;
and I fancy you will have a description which, if not
accurate enough for photography, will, at least, convince you that Nature has hung out the sign of villain in every lineament of the Brute's physiognomy.

Congreve pictured him to the life in his "Double
Dealer:"

"A sedate, a thinking villain, whose black blood
runs temperately bad."

He has a large and active brain—far the most acute
of any that New England has contributed to this war
—a voluble tongue, pleasant voice, and can be, they
say, as gracious, when engaged in a particularly
successful hunt after spoons or specie, as "the mildest-
mannered man that ever cut a throat or scuttled a
ship." But the ineradicable expression of his features must excite suspicion, if not aversion, however
impartial the gazer. It is popularly supposed that his
defect of visual arrangement constitutes his unattrac-
tiveness—but this is a mistake. Mere physical infirm-
ity is only a negative evil to any man, unless it constitutes him a monster. An ugly or deformed man lacks
the indorsement of nature, which smooths the way
for his more favored fellow, but in time he counts for
whatever he is worth. John Wilkes, who was tooth-
less, cross-eyed, and otherwise ugly, was wont to say
(and contemporaries assure us it was no idle boast),
"Give me twenty minutes' conversation, and I will
beat the handsomest man in a race for the favor of the
finest woman in England;" and history is full of celebrated and attractive men, who were cursed with some
personal drawback. Alexander was wry-necked; Cæ

sar, bald; Hannibal and Claudius Civilis, one-eyed; Homer, Milton, and Huber, blind; Beethoven, deaf; Byron, club-footed; Pope and Scarron, horribly crippled; Alcibiades, a stammerer, who could not pronounce "r;" Ovid, abnormal in the nasal department; Mirabeau, pock-marked and "boar-headed;" Attila and Pepin, dwarfs, with enormous cranial developments; Demosthenes, wry-shouldered and a stutterer; Æsop, a hunchback; and the list might be extended to a length extremely consolatory to those of us who would not do for fashion-plates, yet among these were some of the most popular, agreeable, and beloved of the race. In the coruscations of the great tribune's magnetic intellect, women forgot that Mirabeau was a *fright,* as under the witchery of La Valliere's voice, men thought not of her painful lameness. But if Butler were an Antinoüs, with his present *expression* of face, he might reasonably aspire to the presidency of the ugliest of all the ugly clubs. Certainly, he is just the man who would delight to torture women—only, I presume, preferring, if he could have the choice, the plundering of men. Reverdy Johnson hoped to be the Cicero of this Verres, but the catalogue of the satrap's villanies was so black that even his master could not stomach the exposition, and the obnoxious truths were suppressed. The experiment was repeated by a Yankee Virginian, but the Brute laughed at the helpless indignation of his feebler foe, and pursued his speculations and peculations in sublime indifference to all criticism that did not cut off his supplies.

It was only when Smith & Co. threatened, and finally sued him, for the $50,000 in gold he *took* from them, and kept under false pretences, that he roused himself to the exertion of defence—and finally reached the sacrifice of *restitution.*

That he established and maintained order in New Orleans and Norfolk, is undeniable—but it was such order as reigned in Sicily in days of old, and in Warsaw, in later times—the order of sullen, abject, physical fear—a political *coma,* which is itself death, yet in which there was one thing very lively—stealing. The world will never know the truth of this creature's vileness and *success,* until it shall become safe for the hundreds he has robbed and outraged, to tell the story of their wrongs and his robberies. You can hear them in private conversation in Norfolk and New Orleans, from numberless mouths, who now content themselves with whispering what should be proclaimed from house-tops; and yet I sometimes hope he may get his deserts, for even Sherman thinks he will content the homeless, starving wanderers of South Carolina and Georgia, by asking them, as I read in the papers of to-day (January 15, 1866,) how much better off they are than if Butler had the plundering of them!

But I beg unlimited pardon, oh, impatient reader, for all this sermonizing. So, I give my prosy pegasus a rowelling, whereat the old cob frisks his tail, and puts himself out for a faster pace.

Quite a lengthy conversation ensued between myself and Butler—(Mem. I have reflected on the subject and do not think common self-respect will allow me to place his name first)—which proceeded on this wise, the clerk busily recording it all:

"What is your name?"

"Mr. Blank."

"Your profession or pursuit?"

"I am a lawyer."

"You were captured yesterday, near Petersburg?"

"I was."

"How many men were in the trenches with you?"

"About one hundred and twenty or thirty."

"All militiamen?"

"All, with less than half a dozen exceptions."

"And you repulsed, I learn, for two hours, General Kautz's brigade of cavalry?"

"You have been rightly informed."

*   *   *   *   *   *

(Here ensued certain energetic expressions respecting the aforesaid cavalry, which bordered on the extremely profane.)

"Well, Mr. Blank,"—and here he slid forward in his chair, till his head rested on the back, and lit a cigar,—"will you tell me how many soldiers were in Petersburg at the time of General Kautz's first appearance?"

Now the truth was, that to the best of my knowledge and belief, there was not, at that time, in town, as much of a soldier as would entitle the United States Government to declare martial law, and every one knows a half a conscript would serve that purpose. So I bethought me that mystery was my cue, and replied with, I flatter myself, well-affected solemnity:

"I decline answering."

"Oh, you need not decline. I know there was not a soldier there."

"Well, sir, there is no need to ask, if you know; but I am curious to know *how* you know that?"

"By this infallible induction: if there was a soldier in town, no lawyer would get into the trenches!"

I joined in the smile that followed,—and which Butler enjoyed hugely,—more in compliment to the truth than the wit of his inference, and replied:

"You speak of Northern lawyers, I presume. We have contributed our full share to this fight for freedom. If I may speak of myself, I entered the service on the 19th of April, 1861, and thousands of the profession volunteered as early."

"Yes, yes, I understand all that. I volunteered a couple of days before you, but *I never got into the trenches,* and by the help of Heaven I never shall. That is quite another matter, you perceive."

He here took up a note from his desk, held it within four inches of his left eye—what marvel that a man should have a *sinister* expression, whose vision is left-handed?—and   continued:

"I would like to know the position of your government, and particularly of your people, on the subject of negro exchange. I have just received this note from Colonel Ould, in which the question is not met at all, and it is now a month since I applied for a categorical statement of the position of Mr. Davis's government on this topic."

"As I have no official character, I am of course not entitled to speak by authority, and as to the President's individual views, I know nothing."

"Of course, I know you are not a commissioner, but I would be glad to hear your views. I think a white man is as good as a negro, and would be willing to give one of your negroes, if a soldier, for one of my white soldiers. But your government takes the position that the negro is better than a white man, and you will not give up one of my negroes to get back one of your best soldiers."

"My government, I presume, takes no such absurd position—she merely contends that the right of property in a slave is no more affected by his running away to your army, than by his flying to your States,—least of all by your kidnapping. You are entitled to demand the exchange of your negro soldiers, not slaves, just as England would be entitled to claim her Sepoys, and France her Algerines, in the event of war between us and either of those powers. But, both your constitution and your positive statutory enactments, guard the title of the owner against disturbance from any quarter without the jurisdiction of the master's State."

"Ah, yes, but that is the law of peace. You claim the slave as a chattel: now, if I capture land, and it is recaptured, it reverts to the original owner, but if I capture a chattel, a horse for example, on its recapture it becomes the property, *not* of the original owner, but of *your government,* and is doubtless so treated. Thus the capture of *realty* divests title only during occupancy; the capture of *personalty* divests it forever. How do you make the slave an exception?"

"There is plainly no reason, in the nature of things,

why one description of property should be less sacred than another, and the discrimination against personal property only arises, I presume, from the difficulty of identification,—which does not exist in the case of the slave. Hence, the Roman law, if I rightly remember, excepted slaves, and common sense excepts them from the operation of the general rule regarding personalty. So, I presume, would any property be treated that could be easily and certainly identified. For example, a Federal general goes to New Orleans, or Norfolk, and steals my house and all that it contains—furniture, pictures, clothing, jewelry, every thing—but before he has a chance to send them to his wife in Boston or New York, the city is recaptured,—I presume my government would restore me my house with all its contents, and the conquering general would hardly think of holding an auction on my premises."

"I am not certain that he would not have the right. But how do you answer this? Public law authorizes the United States to declare that a slave fleeing to her shall be free: she so does declare in the case of every slave that comes to her."

"I answer that by denial, first of the fact, and then of the right. And though both were true, I do not see how they could affect the power of our own government and laws, to re-establish the original relation, when all parties come again within their jurisdiction."

"Well, sir, it is to be regretted that our governments cannot agree about this, as there will be no more exchanges and no communication till the point is yielded."

"How is it then, general, that while you made

this demand on my government a month ago, you continue to communicate, as I see from Colonel Ould's dispatch?"

"Oh, Mr. Davis moves very slowly, and I was giving him time to make up his mind. He has now had abundant time, and I am going to stop all intercourse."

Our conversation then took quite a wide range, during which I recalled to his memory his own secession at Baltimore, from a certain Democratic convention, and indulged in some references not altogether complimentary to the cruelty and avarice* of certain Federal generals. This seemed to provoke his wrath, and he dismissed me with the emphatic and disagreeable intimation, that my imprisonment would end with the war! *Diis aliter visum,* my dear Brute.

One or two of my comrades were successively ordered into Butler's presence, but his inquiries were few, and chiefly directed to the ascertainment of the force in our city. I do not think he learned much, as we had a little private understanding on this matter beforehand, and we were soon after ordered to "right face" preparatory to a move.

---

* The rapacity of the New England generals is conspicuous. Butler is omnivorous, but Neal Dow's passion was *furniture.* Being quite ill once, one of his officers asked the surgeon who attended him, what was the matter? "Only an unusual meal of furniture; but as I got him to throw up a bureau and a rocking-chair, I think he will recover," was the reply. It was a standing joke among Western soldiers, that General Dow had furniture (as Butler has nigger) on the brain.

CHAPTER V.

To Bermuda Hundreds.—Black-guard.—Awful swearing.—A cold night.—Down the river.—Prison thieves.—Andersonville and Wirz.—Leaving Fortress Monroe.—Maryland.

THE scorching sun was well on the wane when we again struck the trail—this time for Bermuda Hundreds, some two miles off. Sundry mounted officials passed us, wondering very much at the civilian appearance of our squad, and I began then to observe the first indications of the "orderly" epidemic, which I afterwards found to be a universal affliction of the Yankee military. Every one has an "orderly," from the Lieutenant-General, down to the most subordinate pedler in tracts and ginger-bread, that wears the badge of the Sanitary or the Christian Commission. To ride a mile without an obsequious varlet in his wake, whose chief business seems to be to intercept the mud from his horse's heels, is a humiliation which no "free and equal" cavalier of the Great Republic could brook an instant; so, from commissary to commander-in-chief, there's a Sancho for every Don. I attributed this weakness to the novelty of the position of most of these Yanks. To the Southern people their education and labor-system gives the habit of command, and they attach little importance to the possession of a servant, from the generality of the fact of such possession. But most of these democratic centurions never before had the power to say to this one, "Go," and to that one, "Come," and to the other, "Do this;" and as all essentially vulgar minds take delight in the parade of such a power, it is not, perhaps, surprising that many of these Cedrics make a show of their "born thralls" on all occasions; and, sooth to say, Gurth wears his collar with most servile satisfaction.

Past these masters and serfs, past crowds of sutlers and camp followers, past rows of grinning Ethiops, dirty, oleaginous, and idle, we wended our way to the river, which soon was marked out to us by scores on scores of masts; and as twilight fell upon us we arrived in front of a provost-marshal's office, where we answered dutifully to our names, and were turned over to a new authority. A frame building, whose only other tenant was a negro in irons, was allotted to us for the night; and stationing myself in a window, I began, in the little light still left, to amuse myself with drawing a lead-pencil likeness of Butler, when, for the first time, I noticed that our new guards were *black!* An odorous Congo, with a claymore two-thirds his length, a Nubian nose, boundless buttons, and the port of Soulouque, was strutting up and down before me in most amusing enjoyment of his responsible position. Like every other negro soldier I met, with three exceptions, he was as black as Mason's "Challenge," and as surly looking a dog as ever brake bread. Before he had been on duty ten minutes, he picked a quarrel with a brother black who dared to cross his post; and straightway both drew their sabres, to my infinite satisfaction, as I presumed I was about to be favored with a sample of ebony chivalry according to "the code;" but I soon found, to my great grief, that the sabres were only designed to give impetus and a finish to a fusilade of oaths, which, for number, force, and unrelieved profanity, I never heard equalled but once. On our return from Gettysburg, while crossing the mountains, I saw a first-class army "stall,"—scores of wagons blocked up in a narrow mountain-way on a down grade of about two thousand feet to the mile,—every thing with wheels running into every thing else, and a herd of Pennsylvania beeves filling up the small and constantly varying intervals between the vehicles. Then broke forth from the trained lungs and exhaustless vocabulary of a hundred lusty teamsters such a torrent, cataract, avalanche, whirlwind—yea, very "cyclone"—of imprecations as passed competition of the most terrible swearing in Flanders. The common expletives, in which surcharged gall finds vent with ordinary mortals, found no room in that Lodore of cursing—they were obviously thought unworthy the occasion,—and a new set *"horrendum, ingens, informe,"* blasted the ears and eyes, head and heart, legs and body, mane and tail of every individual mule and muleteer in all that involved mass; while the interest of myself and my fellow-soldiers received a spicy fillip from the fact that we had to creep round the edge of this struggling mass, which left but a few inches between the outside rank and an inviting precipice, a half a thousand feet sheer! Then only did I hear superior swearing, before or since, although my experience therein, especially since my capture, has been very large—whereof more anon.

Getting an old stump of a broom, I swept up a small space in one corner of our jail, and, without blanket, or overcoat, laid my head on my arm and was soon asleep. The nights of June are proverbially cool, and our clothing being saturated with perspiration from the heat, exposure, and exercise of the day, I fell into a dream of hunting Frankenstein through the northwest passage, in the midst of which I woke, just in time to save myself from a plunge through a treacherous seal-hole into the Polar Sea! I found myself chilled through and stiff with cold. There was no fire to be had within, and the darkey at the door incontinently refused to permit me to walk out, so I was constrained to restore circulation by certain frantic gymnastics, in which I was, before long, joined by sundry comrades similarly uncomfortable.

Like every thing sublunary (except Coleridge's talks), the night came, perforce, to an end, and we were allowed to go out, two at a time, to wash our faces,—a rather superfluous ceremony in the *absence* of soap and towels, and the most striking *necessity* for both. Salt-junk, coffee, and as much "hard-tack" as we wanted, were issued to us by our "colored brethren," and at eight and a half A. M., a guard of twenty, from the same regiment—the First United States Colored Cavalry—formed around us with drawn swords—a white officer at their head—and, thus convoyed, we proceeded aboard a fine river-boat, the "John A. Warren."

A few minutes after getting aboard, an officer came
from shore with a dispatch from General Butler, commanding the return of three of our party (whom he
designated by name) to his headquarters. This
manœuvre, I believe, never received satisfactory ex-
planation: the men were detained several days by
Butler, and eventually sent to the same prison with
the rest of us. Before another half-hour passed we
heard the tinkle of the engineer's bell, the gang-plank
was drawn aboard, the paddles began to revolve, lines
were cast off, and we felt indeed that we were turning our backs on home. It was the "bluest" moment
of my imprisonment. There seemed such a cruel
injustice in tearing a party of men, some of whose
heads wore the gray honors of many a winter, from
families and friends, and all that men hold dear, for the
crime alone of standing before their own hearths and
homes, and resisting assassins and burglars, bent upon
the desecration of both, that I called in vain on philosophy for consolation, and as we glided along by the
well-remembered and ancient plantations of our beautiful river, seen then the first time for three years,
and to be seen again——alas, when! I recalled the
days when those deserted and wasted mansions, the
homes of the Carters, the Seldens, were the abode
of a courtly, generous hospitality, worthy of the
baronial days of "merrie England," until I filled my
mind and heart with such memories and such regrets
as are wont to moisten sterner eyes than mine.

We sailed past two long pontoon rafts, in preparation for the move of General Grant across the river,
soon to take place with such pomp and trumpeting;

past the cloud of transports, that the supply of his vast army, so soon to change its base, demanded; past the Atlanta, so easily captured not long before in the Savannah; past steamers hurrying to the front with recruits to fill the gaps that Lee's legions were tearing in the Federal lines; and a little before five came abreast of Newport News, and in sight of Old Point and the *resident* fleet of Hampton Roads. When I saw that harbor again, there were two thousaud guns upon it, and such an Armada as the world never saw before. Landed, we were again marched before a provost-marshal, and required to answer our names; and then, under our negro guard, marched to Camp Hamilton, a little west of the large structure formerly known as the Chesapeake Female College, of Hampton.

This "camp" was a two-story wooden barrack, with a small yard, the whole surrounded with a fence some fifteen feet high. Into this inclosure we were marched, our line straightened out, the perennial roll-calling again gone through with; and then we were dismissed, and told to find room to sleep in as best we could.

I had hardly left the ranks when a jolly son of Erin —a Federal soldier—stepped up to me, beckoned me aside, and informed me that the lower story of the building was occupied by Yankee prisoners, incarcerated for various villanies, and that into that apartment I must, under no circumstance, venture, as they garroted and robbed every Confederate soldier they could inveigle into their den. I asked, with some surprise, whether complaint was never made. "Oh, yes," he said, "*greenies* do complain, and the officers laugh in their faces." I needed no further warning, and steered clear of the "below stairs" in that mansion. Five minutes had not elapsed before one of our party emerged from that lower door, swearing like an irate moss-trooper. One of the Yankees had offered him some coffee, for which he was, of course, very grateful, and invited him in to drink it; but he had hardly entered the den before a blanket was thrown over his head, and he was pulled to the earth, his pockets rifled, and even the gold buttons wrenched from his shirt!

This was our first introduction to Yankee privates off duty, and we were not surprised afterwards when we learned that at Andersonville the prisoners had to *hang* a number of their comrades on account of their incorrigible villanies committed against their fellow-prisoners.

I cannot speak of Andersonville, without recalling the monstrous travesty of trial which resulted in the murder of Wirz. That he treated harshly many prisoners, may be true, but when their own fellow-soldiers were compelled in self-defence *to hang some of them* an enemy might be justified in much severity towards them. That Wirz was not the monster whom that scandalous tribunal declared him, is to my mind conclusively proved from a single fact. Hundreds of Federal prisoners were exchanged from Andersonville, and a delegation from the pen went north, to endeavor to induce the Secretary of War to waive for a moment his preference for the negroes, and consent to an exchange. Now, if Wirz had been the murderer which the court-martial declared him, would not

the Northern press, so anxious to catch up any pre-
text for casting odium on the "rebels," and with so
many witnesses of his crimes at hand, have rung with
denunciations of the brutal jailer? Yet, I have never
met ten men North or South, since the evacuation, who
had ever heard the name of Wirz before the surrender! Had he been such a wretch as McNiel or Butler, the whole world would have echoed with denunciations of his name, and he would have been excluded
from all parole.

The crime for which Wirz suffered was failure, and
his hangman was the Republican majorities in New
York and New Jersey. *Mais revenons!*

After this exhibition of the idiosyncrasies of my
enemies I thought it time to get up-stairs among some
honest Confederates, and so mounted to the second
story, where I had the good fortune to meet two old
friends who had been incarcerated there some time,
for the unpardonable offence of running away from
the Confederacy without bringing with them money
enough to convince Butler of their loyalty! Having
been there some time, they had made themselves quite
comfortable, and invited me to a bunk and a good sup-
per, for both of which they have now, as they had then,
my benediction; and having washed my face after a
civilized fashion, I turned in to a sleep which the excitement of the past three days made very desirable
—and very profound. The next day was Sunday, our
first in prison.

"I think that those people, the rituals of whose
churches comprise prayers for the captives, never utter
these petitions with sufficient unction. I'll mend my

fervor in that behalf hereafter." Such is the memorandum in my diary, under date of June 12th. I
commend it, pious reader of mine, to your attention—
make a note on't.

There is in the Roman Catholic Church an order
called the Redemptorists, whose members, besides
taking the usual monastic obligations of poverty, chas-
tity, and obedience, in the early days of the order,
also bound themselves by a vow to dedicate their
lives to the redemption of captives, particularly those
taken by the Moors; and so faithfully did they devote
themselves to this pious vocation, that in the event of
any of them failing to compass otherwise the release
of at least one captive, he considered himself bound
to volunteer to take the place of some Christian prisoner thus confined, and restore him thereby to his
family. Cases of this wonderful self-denial were of
constant occurrence; and, strange to say, the barbarians kept faith with the good monks with surprising
scrupulousness. We concluded while in bonds that
something of that sort was desperately needed at the
present day, if our Federal friends would only be as
honest as the pirates.

About sundown we were marched back to Old
Point, and with a hundred or more compatriots
huddled into the bow of the Louisiana, a well-known
boat of the old Bay line to Baltimore. Here it was
our fortune to succeed, in the tenancy of our premises,
to an invoice of horses brought down by the boat on
her preceding trip; and any thing being thought good
enough for the *rebels,* the ceremonies usual on con-
verting a stable into a human habitation were dis-

pensed with! In these savory quarters we were
packed away; the frowning fortress with her diadem
of cannon soon faded into distance, and by eleven
o'clock we made Point Lookout. Why this cape is
so called I am at a loss to imagine, as there is nothing
in the prospect to make the most curious inhabitant
"look out" in any direction. This matter of nomenclature has puzzled wiser heads than mine, and I am
free to admit that Point Lookout is far from an exceptional case. A certain group of islands in the Pacific
is denominated "Society," because there is no society
there, I suppose; and another denominated "Friendly," although the kindest office the inhabitants perform
to strangers is to eat them. Geography has many a
lucus a non lucendo. The tide being down, we were
landed by means of a little tug that came puffing and
fussing alongside; and hungry, sleepy, and half-frozen,
we set our tired feet on the friendly shores of "Maryland, my Maryland."

CHAPTER VI.

Point Lookout.—A brute.—The Pen.—Lyon's Den.—A friend in need.—The demoralization of prison-life.

It was our misfortune to fall straightway into the hands of a polished scamp—a variety extremely prevalent at Point Lookout, as we afterwards learned. It was scarcely midnight when we landed on a long pier, which jutting out into the Potomac caught the full sweep of the sharp Nor'wester, that screamed and rattled down the channel of the river. The guard, though comfortably clad and furnished with heavy overcoats, suffered acutely; and although the officer who met us as we landed told them that we could not be received until morning, the soldiers did not imagine that their duty required them to stay themselves, or keep their prisoners on the exposed extremity of the long wharf, and they accordingly marched us a few score steps to land. Huddling ourselves together, we were endeavoring to coax a wink from Morpheus, when some ill wind blew the receiving officer, one Lieutenant Phillips, again before us. He straightway opened a torrent of profane abuse upon us and upon our guard, ordered them to take us immediately back to the end of the pier, and waited to see his orders executed, breathing unmentionable execrations against the whole of us. Shivering and utterly miserable, we were marched back, and spent the night in vain efforts to find heat in exercise—sleep being out of the question. The guards themselves, with blanket and overcoat, complained bitterly of the fierce blast; while we had to endure it in light summer costumes, some even without a coat or roundabout. The hours dragged heavily on, and not until seven o'clock in the morning were we allowed to come off the river.

Another provost-marshal's office soon hove in sight, before which we were ranged in a double rank, and the inevitable roll-call again followed. All being right, Lieutenant Phillips, our worthy of the night before, appeared again, rejoicing in mutton-chop whiskers and a grape-vine cane; and, in a gruff, peremptory voice, ordered the first four of us to step out to be searched. This was accomplished by himself and a couple of assistants, and consisted in turning the contents of our pockets on the ground, and then taking off all our clothing, except what was absolutely next the skin, *and part of that also.* This was done to enable the examiners to search thoroughly our persons for money—a commodity which was pretty generally stolen at Point Lookout, either formally or informally—and in ease of Lieutenant Phillips, this ceremony was universally varied by tearing the lining out of the hats and pantaloons of such unfortunates as fell to his lot.

Through indolence or good nature some of the guard discharged this duty too gingerly for this creature's ideas of official obligation, so with a volley of oaths he shouted, "That's no way to search damned rebels;" and proceeded to strip off

3*

the very last garments and tear out the last shred
of lining.

Having thus stolen every thing of any value we had
on our persons, Phillips graciously permitted us to
dress ourselves, and our line being again formed, we
were marched off to "THE PEN."

The military prison, or rather prisons, at Point
Lookout, consisted of two inclosures, the one containing about thirty, the other about ten acres of flat sand,
on the northern shore of the Potomac at its mouth,
but a few inches above high tide, and utterly innocent
of tree, shrub, or any natural equivalent for the same.
Each was surrounded by a fence about fifteen feet
high, facing inwards, around the top of which on the
outer face, and about twelve feet from the ground,
ran a platform on which twenty or thirty sentinels
were posted, keeping watch and ward, night and day,
over the prisoners within. Besides these precautions,
a strongly fortified palisade stretched across the tongue
of land on which the prisons stood, from the bay on
the northeast to the Potomac on the southwest.
Within this palisade, but of course outside of the
"pens," were usually two regiments of infantry, and
a couple of batteries of artillery, and without the forti-
fication two or three companies of cavalry, while,
 riding at anchor in the bay, one gunboat at least was
always to be seen. One face of each of these "pens,"
the eastern, fronted the bay, and gates led from the
inclosures to a narrow belt of land between the fence
and the water, which was free to the prisoners during
the day, piles being driven into the bay on either
hand to prevent any dexterous "reb" from *flanking*

out. A certain portion of the water was marked off by stakes driven into the bottom, for bathing purposes, and most of the prisoners gladly availed themselves of the privilege thus afforded; although, as the same locality precisely and exclusively was devoted to the reception of all the filth of the camp, I admit a squeamishness which deprived me of sea-bathing as long as I stayed there.

Allons, mes amis! we have been outside as long as the gentleman of the grape-vine and mutton-chop will permit—let us enter.

The first thing that struck me as peculiarly prominent within the fence was a row of eight or ten wooden buildings, jutting out from the western face of the pen, a hundred feet long, perhaps, by eighteen in width, and one story high, with four tables running down the entire length of each. At the end next the fence, a partition divided off about twelve feet of the structure. These were the mess-rooms and cook-houses. Here all the public cooking and eating of the premises was conducted. A street, twenty feet in width, ran along the front of these houses, and at right angles to this street were long rows of tents of all imaginable patterns, and of no pattern at all, to within twenty or thirty feet of the opposite face of the inclosure. Each of these rows of tents was designed to contain one thousand prisoners, and at the time of our advent there were ten of these nearly filled, and another just begun. We were assigned to various "divisions," as the rows of tents were called, and dismissed. I was informed that Company "B," fourth division, was my "command," and reporting forthwith to the sergeant of the same, he designated my place as No. 15, in a dirty Sibley tent, which the tenants—from some freak, strongly suggestive of danger, however—had christened and duly labelled, the "Lyon's Den." (I disclaim all responsibility for the orthography.)

I approached the structure with about as heavy a heart as any unregenerate Daniel might be supposed to possess, on presentation to a location with so fearful a name, but the sight that met my eyes as I stooped to pass in, barred my further progress. It is not necessary to enter more particularly into details, than to intimate that my prospective messmates were anxiously on the war-path after certain animals of the parasite order, whose name—*infandum*—has the same origin as that of *la belle passion!*

Marius, amid the ruins of Carthage; Belisarius, begging the obolus; Coriolanus, when his ma was plaguing him, or Miss Gunnybags, in the first instant of her discovery that Flora McF.'s face was a half-inch deeper than her own—not the grief of any or all of these (except possibly the last), could equal the mute misery with which—hungry, sleepy, dirty, tired, angry, robbed, and rebellious, I stalked away (if five feet eight and a half *can* stalk), with a sigh and a groan, from the "Lyon's Den."

I had not gone far before I was hailed by name in a voice perfectly familiar, though I had not heard it before for some time, and, turning in the direction whence it came, saw a well-known face, my *vis-d-vis* aforetime in many a game of "prisoner's base," or "chermany," in the blissful days of boyhood. I think he must have known intuitively both the character and the depth of my misery; for his first question was: "Where are your quarters?" Quarters, indeed! I had rather be quartered, hanged, and drawn besides, than to have passed my time as No. 15 in the *den* aforementioned. I mentioned the dread name with a sickly attempt at a smile, which was a signal failure, when my friend, a ten months' resident of the prison, invited me around to his *shebang (Anglice,* domicile) until I could better provide myself.

I wended my way thither assailed by sights and smells as numerous and noxious as Coleridge found in the savory descendant of Colonia Agrippina, and in ten seconds—such is the expedition of prison etiquette—was made acquainted with, and on the most social terms with such of my comrade's friends as I had not before known.

Sleep was what I wanted most, so borrowing a blanket from my good Samaritan, I availed myself of his invitation, and before many minutes was happily indifferent to all terrestrial affairs. Physiologists have amused themselves with recording the order in which the several senses go to sleep: my own opinion is that, under such circumstances, they make a lumping business of it, and fall by platoons; certainly such was my experience.

I now began prison-life in earnest, and none but those who have experienced it can approximate an idea of its wretchedness. This does not consist in loss of liberty, in absence from home, in subjection to others' control, in insufficient food, in scant clothing, in loss of friends, in want of occupation, in an exposed

life, in the absence of all conveniences of living. God
knows, all these are bad enough, and contribute in the
aggregate greatly to the enhancement of the misery
of a prisoner. I think, however, that the great over-
shadowing agony of imprisonment, to persons of any
culture, is isolation—

> "the dreary void,
> The leafless desert of the mind,
> The waste of feelings unemployed."

The world, friends, fellow-citizens, home, are things as
remote as though in another sphere. Death brings
its compensation, aside from the consolations of religion, in the remembrance that it is irreversible, and
we choke down and eradicate, if we cannot exalt and
purify those emotions, whereof the lost were the objects, insensibly changing our social schedule to meet
the new order of things. But the prisoner preserves
affections and interests without being able to indulge
them, and thus with straining eyes and quickening
pulse, he dismisses continually the dove for the expected emblem, but it returns forever with flagging
wing and drooping head, not having found whereon
to rest its weary foot. Thus, there comes that despair which is the aggregate of many, or the suprem-
acy of one disappointment—and from despair comes
always degradation. Men become reckless, because
hopeless—brutalized, because broken-spirited, until
from disregard of the formalities of life, they become
indifferent to its duties, and pass with rapid though
almost insensible steps from indecorum to vice—until
a man will pick your pocket in a prison, who would
sooner cut his own throat at home.

The evidence of the prisoners at Andersonville establishes this, and confirms the unanimous experience of those who have passed any time in confinement. The men there, became such utter outlaws, that the prisoners were compelled to organize themselves into vigilance committees and deal swift and mortal vengeance on their murderous companions.

As I believe there never was in the Confederate army any such body of thieves, and ravishers, and house-burners, and hardened wretches, as the "bummers" of Sherman's host, so I doubt if such a set of outlaws ever assembled in any prison as were congregated at Andersonville; yet that which happened there occurred, if not with the same flagrancy, wherever large numbers of prisoners have been congregated.

To assemble large numbers of men in crowded quarters, apart from the restraints of home and friends and female society, and so keep them for months deprived of sufficient food for body or mind, and with no employment except at rare intervals, or in exceptional cases, and deprived also of liberty, is certain to make them hogs, and very likely to make them devils,

CHAPTER VII.

Order of exercises.—Fabrications of the Sanitary Commission—
History of the pen.—Official clothes thieves.—The guards.—
Blackguards again.

THE routine of prison-life at Point Lookout was as
follows. Between dawn and sunrise a "reveille" horn
summoned us into line by companies, ten of which
constituted each division—of which I have before
spoken—and here the roll was called. This performance was hurried over with as much haste as is ascribed
to certain marital ceremonies in a poem that it would
be obviously improper to make a more particular allusion to; and those whose love of a nap predomi-
nates over fear of the Yankees, usually tumble in for
another snooze. About eight o'clock the breakfasting
began. This operation consisted in the forming of the
companies again into line, and introducing them under
lead of their sergeants into the mess-rooms, where a
slice of bread and a piece of pork or beef—lean in the
former and fat in the latter being contraband of war—
were placed at intervals of about twenty inches apart.
The meat was usually about four or five ounces in
weight. These we seized upon, no one being allowed
to touch a piece, however, until the whole company
entered, and each man was in position opposite his ration (universally pronounced *raytion,* among our ene-

mies, as it is almost as generally called with the "a" short among ourselves, symbolical, you observe, of the *shortness* of provant in Dixie). This over, a detail of four or five men from each company—made at morning roll-call—formed themselves into squads for the cleansing of the camp; an operation which the Yankees everywhere attend to with more diligence than ourselves. The men then busied themselves with the numberless occupations which the fertility of American genius suggests, of which I will have something to say hereafter, until dinner-time, when they were again carried to the mess-houses, where another slice of bread, and rather over a half-pint of watery slop, by courtesy called "soup," greeted the eyes of such ostrich-stomached animals as could find comfort in that substitute for nourishment.

About sunset, at the winding of another horn, the roll was again called, to be sure that no one had "flanked out," and, about an hour after, came "taps;" after which, all were required to remain in their quarters, and keep silent.

The Sanitary Commission, a benevolent association of exempts in aid of the Hospital Department of the Yankee army, published in July 1865 a "Narrative of Sufferings of United States Officers and Soldiers, Prisoners of War," in which a parallel is drawn between the treatment of prisoners on both sides, greatly to the disadvantage, of course, of "Dixie."

An air of truthfulness is given to this production by a number of affidavits of Confederate prisoners, which made many a Confederate stare and laugh to read.

They were generally the statements of "galvanized"

rebels, "so called;" that is, prisoners who had applied
for permission to take the oath, or of prisoners who
had little offices in the various pens, which they would
lose on the whisper of any thing disagreeable, and
their testimony is entitled to the general credit of depp-
ositions taken "under duress."

But among these documentary statements, in glori-
fication of the humanity of the Great Republic, is one
on page 89, from Miss Dix, the grand female dry-nurse
of Yankee Doodle (who, by the by, gave, I understand,
unpardonable offence to the pulchritude of Yankeedom, by persistently *refusing to employ any but ugly
women as nurses*—the vampire)—which affirms that
the prisoners at Point Lookout "were supplied with
vegetables, with the best of wheat bread, and fresh
and salt meat three times daily in abundant measure."

Common gallantry forbids the characterization of
this remarkable extract in harsher terms than to say
that it is untrue *in every particular.*

It is quite likely that some Yankee official at Point
Lookout made this statement to the benevolent itine-
rant, and her only fault may be in suppressing the fact
that she *"was informed,"* etc., etc. But it is altogether inexcusable in the Sanitary. Commission to
attempt to palm such a falsehood upon the world,
knowing its falsity, as they must have done. For my
part, I never saw any one get enough of any thing to
eat at Point Lookout, except the soup, and a tea-
spoonful of that was *too much* for ordinary digestion.

These digestive discomforts were greatly enhanced
by the villanous character of the water, which is so
impregnated with some mineral as to offend every

nose, and induce diarrhæa in almost every alimentary canal. It colors every thing black in which it is allowed to rest, and a scum rises on the top of a vessel if it is left standing during the night, which reflects the prismatic colors as distinctly as the surface of a stagnant pool. Several examinations of this water have been made by chemical analysis, as I was told by a Federal surgeon in the prison, and they have uniformly resulted in its condemnation by scientific men; but the advantages of the position to the Yankees, as a prison pen, so greatly counterbalanced any claim of humanity, that Point Lookout I felt sure would remain a prison camp until the end of the war, especially as there are wells outside of "the Pen," which are not liable to these charges, the water of which is indeed perfectly pure and wholesome, so that the Yanks suffer no damage therefrom. The ground was inclosed at Point Lookout for a prison in July, 1863, and the first instalment of prisoners arrived there on the 25th of that month from the Old Capitol, Fort Delaware, and Fort McHenry, some of the Gettysburg captures. One hundred and thirty-six arrived on the 31st of the same month from Washington, and on the 10th of August another batch came from Baltimore, having been captured at Falling Water. Every few weeks the number was increased, until they began to count by thousands.

During the scorching summer, whose severity during the day is as great on that sand-barren as anywhere in the Union north of the Gulf, and through the hard winter, which is more severe at that point than anywhere in the country south of Boston, these poor fellows were confined here in open tents, on the naked ground, without a plank or a handful of straw between them and the heat or frost of the earth.

And when, in the winter, a high tide and an easterly gale would flood the whole surface of the pen, *and freeze as it flooded,* the sufferings of the half-clad wretches, many accustomed to the almost vernal warmth of the Gulf, may easily be imagined. Many died outright, and many more will go to their graves crippled and racked with rheumatisms, which they date from the winter of 1863—4. Even the well-clad sentinels, although relieved every thirty minutes (instead of every two hours, as is the army rule), perished in some instances, and in others lost their feet and hands, through the terrible cold of that season.

During all this season the ration of wood allowed to each man was an arm-full for five days, and this had to cook for him as well as warm him, for at that time there were no public cook-houses and mess-rooms.

An additional refinement of cruelty was the regulation which always obtained at Point Lookout, and which I believe was peculiar to the prison, under which the Yanks-stole from us any bed-clothing we might possess, *beyond one blanket!* This petty larceny was effected through an instrumentality they call *inspections.* Once in every ten days an inspection was ordered, when all the prisoners turned out in their respective divisions and companies *in marching order.* They ranged themselves in long lines between the rows of tents, with their blankets and haversacks —those being the only articles considered orthodox possessions of a rebel. A Yankee inspected each man, taking away his extra blanket, if he had one, and appropriating any other superfluity he might chance to possess; and this accomplished, he visited the tents and seized every thing therein that under, the convenient nomenclature of the Federals was catalogued as "contraband"—blankets, boots, hats, any thing. The only way to avoid this was by a judicious use of greenbacks—and trifle would suffice,—it being true, with honorable exceptions, of course, that Yankee soldiers are very much like ships: to move them, you must "slush the ways."

In the matter of clothing, the management at Point Lookout was simply infamous. You could receive nothing in the way of clothing without giving up the corresponding article which you might chance to possess; and so rigid was this regulation, that men who came there barefooted have been compelled to beg or buy a pair of worn-out shoes to carry to the office in lieu of a pair sent them by their friends, before they could receive the latter. To what end this plundering was committed I could never ascertain, nor was I ever able to hear any better, or indeed any other reason advanced for it, than that the possession of extra clothing would enable the prisoners to bribe their guards! Heaven help the virtue that a pair of second-hand Confederate breeches could seduce!

As I have mentioned the guards, and as this is a mosaic chapter, I may as well speak here as elsewhere of the method by which order was kept in camp. During the day, the platform around the pen was constantly paced by sentinels, chiefly of the Invalid (or, as it is now called, the Veteran Reserve) Corps,

whose duty it was to see that the prisoners were
orderly, and particularly, that no one crossed "the
dead-line." This is a shallow ditch traced around
within the inclosure, about fifteen feet from the fence.
The penalty for stepping over this is death, and although the sentinels are probably instructed to warn
any one who may be violating the rule, the order
does not seem to be imperative, and the negroes, when
on duty, rarely troubled themselves with this superfluous formality. Their warning was the click of the
lock, sometimes the discharge of their muskets. These
were on duty during my stay at the Point every third
day, and their insolence and brutality were intolerable.

Besides this detail of day-guard, which of course
was preserved during the night, a patrol made the
rounds constantly from "taps," the last *horn* at night,
to "reveille." These were usually armed with pistols
for greater convenience, and as they are shielded from
scrutiny by the darkness, the indignities and cruelties they oftentimes inflicted on prisoners, who for
any cause might be out of their tents between those
hours, especially when the patrol were black, were
outrageous. Many of these were of a character which
could not by any periphrase be decently expressed,—
they were, however, precisely the acts which a set of
vulgar brutes, suddenly invested with irresponsible
authority, might be expected to take delight in; and,
as it was of course impossible to recognize the perpe-
trators, redress was unattainable, even if one could
brook the sneer and insult which would inevitably follow complaint. Indeed, most of the Yankees did not
disguise their delight at the insolence of these Congoes.

CHAPTER VIII.

Shelter at Point Lookout.—Cracker-box houses.—A prison adventure.—Prison ingenuity.—The washerwomen.—Contributions to prisoners.—The war a people's war.—A woman.—A loyal negro.

I HAVE said that the only shelter supplied by the Yankee government to the prisoners at Point Lookout was canvas. Tents were issued to the prisoners at the rate of one "A tent"—covering about six feet square—to each squad of *five;* or one Sibley tent—covering a circle whose diameter is about fifteen feet—to every eighteen men. The camp uniformity was, however, agreeably diversified by mansions of aristocratic proportions and finish, which from their material were styled "cracker-box houses." Top-boots and a cracker-box house fill the measure of any genuine Point Lookouter's ambition. To want these, was to be the *subject* of envy—to possess them, was to be its *object* (I speak Kant—as many a better man before me). It was only as a very special favor that a rebel was allowed to wear boots there at all, but the other blessing being attainable by all by means of a little cash and much diligence, was a lawful object of universal ambition. They were made on this wise:

A large proportion of the bread used at all prisons consists of square crackers made of flour, water, and salt alone, and thoroughly baked, which are put up

in fifty-pound boxes, and everywhere denominated
"hard-tack." The boxes in which these crackers are
packed, are made of white pine or some other light
and easily-worked wood, and are, I suppose, about
thirty-two inches long, by twenty broad and twelve
deep. They are the perquisites of the prison commissary, who sells them at from ten to fifteen cents
apiece, according to the demand. These were knocked
to pieces carefully, the nails all saved, and the boards
put away, until longer pieces of wood in sufficient
numbers to make a frame were procured from outside. This accomplished, and the boards nailed on
carefully, the "A tent" was slit up the back, and
stretched across the ridge pole of the new domicile to
form the roof. If newspapers, especially illustrated
ones, could be procured, the walls were papered in-
side, increasing the comfort as well as bettering the
appearance of the room; a fireplace was made in the
end, of sun-dried bricks of home manufacture, which
having been raised four or five feet, was surmounted
by a flour-barrel; the floor was spread with sand
from the beach, a table and a couple of chairs were
improvised, bunks constructed, a name painted (with
a composition of soot and vinegar) over the door; and
the family moved in—men of mark and consequence
forever thenceforth in the chronicles of Point Lookout!

Most of these buildings were put up by Marylanders, whose proximity to their homes enabled them to
command a larger exchequer than the other prisoners,
and they were very creditable specimens of the taste,
ingenuity, and industry of artificers, whose only tools

usually were a jackknife and a piece of the iron hoop of a beef-barrel filed into the semblance of a saw.

Many of the names by which these mansions were designated were purely fanciful, as, "Here's your Mule," "The Alhambra," etc., but sometimes they were more significant. I noticed a very neat one at the end of the division in which I slept, labelled "Home Again;" and on inquiry learned that the appropriateness of the title depended on the following incident. It was erected on the ground of a former structure of the same kind, tenanted by the same parties, which came to grief as follows. Its occupants, an ingenious party with considerable mechanical skill, had contrived to accumulate cracker-box lumber in large quantities without exciting suspicion, under pretence of building a larger house; and by watching their opportunities, had fashioned their material into two canoes, each capable of containing two or three men. These boats could be carried under the arm, the various parts disjointed, without exciting suspicion; and could be readily fitted together, even in the dark, by those who were familiar with their construction. Every thing promised success, and they were awaiting a night of favoring darkness, having made the necessary arrangements for getting outside of the inclosure—that is to say, bribed the guard. In their frail boats they had resolved to trust themselves, for love of sweet liberty, to the mercy of the river, which at its mouth is exceedingly rough, when, unfortunately, the Yanks got wind of the daring project. They sent a guard to the house, found the canoes, made a bonfire of them, and then razed the castle to the ground, leaving not a bit of it standing, "from turret to foundation-stone." For some time the baffled tenants wandered around, pensioners upon the charity of their comrades; but at last they ventured on rebuilding their palace, and having accomplished this unmolested, they gave modest vent to their satisfaction, as well as a visiting card to their friends, by writing over their door, "Home Again."

As I have spoken of the architectural performances of the "rebs," I may as well do scant justice here as elsewhere to the surprising ingenuity and skill displayed by them in the various devices with which they contrived to beguile the tedium (and buy the tobacco) of prison-life.

The larger portion of the manufactures of the prisoners consisted of rings, chains, breastpins, shirt buttons, lockets, etc., of gutta-percha. These were beautifully carved, in an infinite diversity of style and design; and inlaid with gold, silver, and pearl, in an endless variety of ornamental device. The rings were chiefly made of coat-buttons; the chains exclusively, I believe, from a certain long hollow tube of gutta-percha, used as a needle in some description of knitting or crochet, by sawing the cylinder into rings, slitting one side of each, and thus linking them together; and the other ornaments were made principally of what is known as block gutta-percha, the masses of which, being of greater thickness, afforded the means of heavier work. A large needle, to drill the holes for the pins which confine the inlaid material, a hand-lathe which was easily made in a half-hour, and a knife, one blade of which was filed into a saw, were the only instruments required for this manufacture, though many who had been long at the business had supplied themselves with graver's tools of every variety.

A more ambitious class of workmen confined themselves to carving in bone; and I remember a "Greek Slave," a "Paul in chains,"* and a "crucifix," by one of these, which would not shame an experienced artist, and yet the maker had never carved a pipe, even, until he was a prisoner. I feel no hesitation in mentioning the name of the ingenious gentleman who wrought thus beautifully, nor any delicacy in giving this public expression to the hope that Mr. W. W. Marstellar will do himself and his native State, Virginia, the justice to cherish and mature the talent he so obviously possesses in unusual degree.

While these were the regular occupations of camp, no division was without one or two shoemakers, and as many tailors and barbers, who contrived somehow to obtain both the tools and materials of their trades; while here and there throughout the camp, you would find gingerbread and molasses-candy of domestic manufacture for sale, and, strangely enough, one or two regular eating-houses, where a very respectable dinner could be obtained for fifty cents! The solvent power of money triumphs over every obstacle.

---

*This carving ("Paul") was subsequently presented by Mr. Marstellar to General Robert E. Lee through General (and then Governor) William Smith of Virginia, in whose command Mr. M. formerly was, and the old general acknowledged it in a handsome autograph note which the donor prizes above all his handiwork.

Well and wisely wrote that rollicking son of Venu-sium:

_____"rem   facias: rem

Si possis recte, si non, quocunquo modo rem."

For with that useful _rem_ what has not been and may not be accomplished.

Before my arrival at Point Lookout, two of its most celebrated pieces of workmanship had been sold out-side. One of these was a locomotive, with a camp-kettle for a boiler, and the other a watch, which filled a common canteen! both of which worked admirably, as I learned from many who inspected them. The handsomest, and, considering all the difficulties, the most surprising sample of mere mechanical ingenuity which I saw, was a violin made of a cracker-box, wherein all the curves and undulations of that preter-naturally twisted instrument were reproduced with the utmost fidelity. This curiosity stood the crucial test of practice, for I had the pleasure of hearing as honest a jig extracted from its sonorous body as ever tried the endurance or evidenced the skill of dame or dem-oiselle in all the tide of time.

The locomotive was, as I learned, purchased for Barnum's Museum—such, at least, was the belief in-side the pen; so, I presume, it was resolved into its original elements in that terrible fire, so eloquently and accurately described by the New York _World,_ when the mermaid had her tail burnt to a cinder before she knew she was a-fire, and the whale was devoured in a sauce made principally of his own spermaceti, after having been boiled to unusual liveliness in his narrow tank.

Another source of extensive profits in prison was the pursuit of the washerwomen—if that phrase may be used without compromising the conscript liability of the subjects. The labors of these useful *ouvriers* were conducted on the beach at low tide. The beating of the waves against the bank, which is formed just here of a tenacious clay, leaves a little bluff some two or three feet high, along the bay face of the prison, which, as I have before mentioned, was free to the prisoners during the day. Here the washers most did congregate. Their first duty was to make a stove. This was effected by digging a round hole in this clay bluff, about eight inches in diameter, and as many deep, the outer rim of which was some four or five inches from the edge of the bluff. A second hole was then tunnelled in the face of the bluff, at such a distance below the surface as would allow it to strike the bottom of the first hole, so that the two apertures had the general form of the elbow of a stove-pipe; and the furnace was complete. A fire was made in the larger cavity, over the mouth of which the boiler was placed, being raised form the ground by a few pebbles that the draught might be perfect. The washerwoman rolled up his pants, and waded out a few yards, to clear water, filled his bucket with the salt tide, and was soon under weigh.

The washerwoman did not, however, monopolize this belt of ground, unfortunately. Its most numerous occupants were *gumblers,* who, under hastily constructed booths, which they erected every morning, and slept on every night, carried on every game of cards at which money is staked, from aristocratic "faro" to cut-throat *monte*. Here the dice rattled, and the cards were shuffled from morning till night; every thing representing value, from a "hard-tack" up, being freely offered and accepted as legitimate currency. In truth, the "hard-tack" may be considered the unit of value in prison. One of them would purchase a single chew of tobacco anywhere in camp; eight would buy a United States postage stamp; ten, a loaf of bread, etc. Indeed, the air resounded, from rosy morn to dewy eve, with such sounds as, "Here's yer tobaccer for yer hard-tack." "Here's envelopes for yer hard-tack," and the like. There was quite an amount of this commodity always in circulation, from the fact that many of the prisoners were not dependent on the Government rations; so they drew their supplies, and either gave them, or sold them, to less fortunate neighbors.

Whence came the money for all this gambling you naturally ask, and I confess I was for a long time puzzled by the phenomenon. The regulations of this prison not only prescribed that all money should be taken from prisoners on their entry, but that, under no circumstances, should money be delivered to them. When friends, therefore, transmitted them supplies of this sort, they were taken possession of by the commandant of the camp, who notified the prisoner, and the latter was then permitted, in one form or another, to draw on the deposit thus made. At Point Lookout, under the *régime* at the time of our capture, the money was issued in sutler's checks or tickets, which the sutler was forbidden to receive again from any one not a prisoner. Subsequently, the plan was de-

vised of handing to each prisoner who had money to
his credit, a pass-book, on the first page of which he
found himself credited with the money sent him, and
debited with the cost of the book, and by taking this
account-book to the sutler, purchases could be effected
to the amount of the balance due. But, under whatever form, *money obtained, by some means, admission.*
Rebel ingenuity managed it, and I am overwhelmed
with regret, oh, most indulgent of readers, that "the
exigencies of the public service" do not permit me to
say *how.* I know you are not satisfied, but "odds
bodikins!" how can I help that? Curiosity has
brought many a man and woman to condign grief
since our common grandmother's unfortunate *esca-
pade,* and, doubtless, will continue to be the vestibule
to misery till the crack of doom. Ruminate thereon,
and be comforted, for tell you, I am resolved beyond
hope of repentance, I will not.

The fact of its receipt constituted the great difference between the prisoners of the two peoples. A
Federal prisoner had no sympathy arising from any
other sentiment than mere humanity at the South.
The war was the war of the people. In it every hope
and interest and energy and affection of a brave people were centred. The effort to prejudice the cause of
the South by declaring the war to have been the act
of a few discontented politicians, was necessary to jus-
tify the North before the eyes of the world. If it had
once been admitted that *the people* of ten States with
great unanimity desired independence, the unexampled
wickedness of a war for their subjugation by a people
themselves the creation of a revolution which asserted

the people's right to change their governments at will, would have been manifest to the world. Hence the ear of the earth was filled with the averment that the people had no heart in the war. But no assertion was ever more false. Like every other war ever begun in earth's history, the *people* did not *originate* it, but no war in history ever was so popular when once begun. Its failure was the crushing by brute force of the aspiration of eight millions of people for liberty, and history will so record it.

The war-party in the Union *now* admit it, because it is now their *interest* to do so. They declare that there is no true Union sentiment in the South; that no Union man can be elected to any office; that the rebels are subjugated, not converted; that the mass of the people are sullenly hostile to the Union. What is all this but a proclamation to the world that the Southern war for liberty was *the people's war,* and that the North, in liberating four millions of blacks, enslaved eight millions of whites?

This plain view of the matter was taken by many thousands in the North, and was expressed while expression was free. After a while, Seward's little bell began to tinkle; and the holders of obnoxious opinions were Bastiled into silence, if not orthodoxy.

But one method of expression was left open, and freely availed of—*charity to the prisoners.* It was noble, princely—divine. Insult, outrage, imprisonment, threats—nothing could stem this noble tide, until the generous, liberal, magnanimous Federal Government *forbade the Express companies to carry packages for rebel prisoners!*

If the prayers and gratitude of thousands of men and thousands of women and children, widows many and orphans, could reward the noble people in the Northern States who thus gave their testimony for the great right of self-government, they have it a thousand-fold—there is nothing else left us with which to make a return.

In the South, on the other hand, every Yankee soldier was looked on as a foe who had invaded our homes to enslave us. We tried to impose no government on them; they were attempting to force one upon us. We disclaimed in the heydey of our fortunes any purpose but separation; they everywhere and always proclaimed their design to be, to force us into a union with them. We assured them we abhorred that union: they thirsted for the unwilling embrace.

It is not much wonder, then, that there was no individual sympathy for those who were captives among us, and that when the Government issued rations to them such as it had to give, they were dependent on that alone for subsistence.

Revenons! I must not forget to mention that among the convicts was a woman! She was captured in the Valley of Virginia, I was informed, while acting as a member of an artillery company, and her sex discovered, probably, on the usual search for valuables. Common civility suggested a conversation with her; and one day as I was passing the little tent which was assigned to her exclusively, I approached her for the purpose of making some inquiries, as well as letting her know that we were disposed to serve her in

4*

any way possible to prisoners. She seemed, however, indisposed to converse, and I was compelled to give up the chase. Why the Yanks detained her I can't imagine, as I believe, in the rare instances in which these Amazonian propensities had brought the sex to trouble theretofore, on either side, their exchange was promptly made.

Another *"rara avis"*—the remainder of the line is even more pointedly appropriate—*"nigroque simillima cycno"*—was a genuine "Old Virginny" negro, named "Dick," whilom a servant at the Bollingbrook Hotel in Petersburg, who was taken while in the service as cook to some mess, during the Gettysburg campaign. Dick had been importuned, time and again, to renounce the Confederate cause, come out of prison and accept work and good wages outside; but he resisted with Roman fortitude—protested that he was a "Jeff. Davis" man, that he was going back to his home, and wanted nothing to do with the Yankees.

Dick's loyalty to his section, tempted and persecuted as he was on all sides, and especially by the negro soldiers when on duty, was very exhilarating. It involved, of course, many sacrifices; but Dick rose superior to them all, sublimely indifferent to all mortal woes except such as are supposed to be inseparable from the pursuits of any honest washerwoman—that being Dick's profession.

Dick remained a prisoner until near the end of the war, having been in durance twenty months, and is now at his old home in Petersburg, where we hope he may live long and happily. The advent of our party was to him a source of mingled mortification and delight.

He obviously regretted to see us in bonds, but he was glad to hear news of many who had been dead to him for a year, and his gratification took the practical turn of placing his purse and labor at our disposal.

Day now followed day in tedious progression, little occurring to break the monotony of a life which has all the stupidity of a tread-mill without its exercise. The few incidents that marked it, I cannot, perhaps, more conveniently dispose of than by extracting from my diary, with a little amplification for greater clearness.

CHAPTER IX.

Black patriots on the rampage.—Major Weymouth's inspection.—
Foul water.—Columbia.—Rumored capture of Petersburg.—Peculiar costume.—The rationale of rations.

Thursday, June 16*th.*—A prisoner a week to-day—
it seems a year. Last night the negro regiment which
constitutes part of our guard, and which has been
raiding over in Westmoreland and the adjacent counties, returned with great beating of drums and blowing of fifes. The captives of these brave soldiers of
the Republic consisted of a hundred head of cattle—
principally poor women's cows—several ploughs, bug-
gies, primeval sulkies, harrows, beds, chairs, etc., and
from twenty to thirty decrepit citizens! This is the
service in which these demons are regularly employed.
Every month, and sometimes more frequently than
once in thirty days, they are sent across the river on
a plundering tour. The Yankees are too much
ashamed of this to fill their papers with the doings of
these valiant "swash bucklers," but they are glad of
the means of keeping alive, by this promise of stated
plunderings, the *martial ardor* and *fidelity* of their
black brethren, and, of course, are not unwilling to
share the spoils. These raids, which were usually
made in a country entirely devoid of Confederate
soldiers, are, of course, without any earthly justifica-

tion or purpose, except to gratify the malignity and
feed the beastliness of their new allies, whose delight
in these safe robberies is, as may be expected, boundless. The old men are usually kept a short time in an
uninclosed camp outside, under guard of the negroes,
and then returned to their homes, the Yankees even
not having the audacity to detain them—perhaps not
the humanity to feed them. These thieves were generally accompanied by a Doctor——, and those who
knew him in the prison spoke very indignantly of the
vulgar boasts they ascribed to him on his return, of
the plunder he seized.

Saw to-day, for the first time, the chief provost-
marshal, Major H.G.O. Weymouth. He is a handsome official, with ruddy face, a rather frank countenance, and a cork-leg. He conducts this establishment on the *"laissez faire"* principle—in short, he
lets it alone severely. Whatever the abuses or complaints, or reforms, the only way to reach him is by
communications through official channels, said channels being usually the authors of the abuses! It may
be easily computed how many documents of this
description would be likely to meet his eye.

Two or three times a week he rides into camp with
a sturdy knave behind him, at a respectful distance—
makes the run of one or two streets, and is gone, and
I presume sits down over a glass of brandy and water,
and indites a most satisfactory report of the condition
of the "rebs," for the perusal of his superior officer,
or plies some credulous spinster with specious fictions
about the comfort, abundance, and general desirable-
ness of Yankee prisons. Major bears a bad reputa-

tion here, in the matter of money; all of which, I
presume, arises from the unreasonableness of the
"rebs," who are not aware that they have no rights
which Yankees are bound to respect.

Friday, June 17th.—A salute of thirteen guns heralded this morning the arrival of General Augur, who
commands the department of Washington. About
twelve M., the general, with a few other officials, made
the tour of camp, performing, in the prevailing per-
functory manner, the official duty of inspection.

Nothing on earth can possibly be more ridiculous
and absurd than the great majority of official inspections of all sorts; but this "banged Bannagher." General Augur did not speak to a prisoner, enter a tent,
peep into a mess-room, or, so far as I saw, take a single
step to inform himself how the pen was managed.

Weymouth probably fixed up a satisfactory report,
however, when the general's brief exhibition of his
new uniform to the appalled "rebs" was over.

Visited all my comrades to-day, and, with one exception, found them all suffering like myself from
exhausting diarrhœa, induced by the poisonous water.

Sunday, June 19th. —The New York papers received to-day are blatant with accounts, most detailed
and circumstantial, of the capture of Petersburg. The
back-door of Richmond is now secured, say the editors, and bets are freely offered in Grant's army, according to the correspondents, that the "Fourth of
July" will be celebrated under the shadow of Washington's statue, on Capitol Square, in Richmond! All
this I believe, with unhesitating faith, to be a lie of
the first-water, explicable alone in the light of the cir-

cumstance, that *the regular mail for Europe left yes-*
terday. Such of General Grant's officers as celebrate
the next "Fourth" in Richmond, will perform that
patriotic service in the Libby, and to-morrow's papers
(the steamer being gone) will contradict the falsehood
of to-day. And yet—here's the psychological paradox
in the matter—the credulous Yanks, though thus de-
ceived, on a moderate calculation, three hundred and
sixty-five times in every year of grace since the war
began, are as ready now to be deluded as in the earliest hour of the earliest day, and the enterprising
geniuses who control, or furnish news for, the press
of the North, play the game of wholesale lying, with
the same profound audacity and superb success this
blessed day, as when they first gave American circulation to the European simile, "Lying like a bulletin."
Mein Gott yot a beebles!

To-day we were blessed with our first practical experience of the beauties of a Yankee inspection. The
massacre of the innocent (blankets) was wholesale and
very provoking. I performed an acceptable service
for a fellow-prisoner, by appearing in line with his
extra blanket in my hand, not having one of my own.
Our division being a new one—for though sleeping in
the Fourth, I answered roll in the Twelfth—the prisoners had but little superfluous cloth of any sort, and the
Yank who did the stealing from us, was obviously
mortified at the scant game he bagged.

While waiting dutifully, hour by hour, for our in-
spector to approach and perform his task, the gates of
the prison opened, and a batch of "rebs," numbering
a couple of hundred, entered. Among them were sev-

eral of our fellow-citizens of Petersburg, captured in
the attack of the preceding Thursday, I believe, by
Baldy Smith and Hancock, which gave rise to the
flaming particulars of the capture of the gallant Cockade, so ostentatiously displayed in the journals of Saturday. They assure us that our little city is still safe,
but the accounts they bring of the distress of the inhabitants, on the day after our capture, are heart-
rending. I can well imagine it. Only a drop it was,
truly, in that fierce tide, each refluent wave of which
comes to the shore of the South crested with the
shattered wrecks of the best, and dearest, and noblest
of her sons; yet to those mourning homes in Petersburg, shuddering with the agony of an unexpected
and bloody woe, that drop was a consuming flood.
Her young men had gone into the war with a noble
prodigality of their lives, and health, and comfort,
that proved them worthy of the ancient fame of their
little city, and of the priceless heritage they coveted;
and when they fell, they were mourned indeed, but it
was a sacrifice anticipated and in some sort prepared
for. But on that day, the fathers and grandfathers
fell—the bullet cheated the grave. The blood-stained
locks were gray—the pallid cheeks were *wrinkled.*
It was not mothers that wailed the lost, but daughters and daughters' daughters! Yet, how well and
worthily these heroes shed their blood, let the record
of the villanies now staining, as I write, the track of
Sherman, attest!

These lines were written with the news of the
doings of the drunken fiends in Columbia before my
eyes. When the terror of prison and fire is raised

from Southern pens, let some South Carolinian, whose sick wife was taken on a sheet from her bed and laid in a gutter by *humane* soldiers, while their comrades tore the earrings from her bleeding ears, and prayed her to look what a fine blaze her house was making, write the record of that great campaign. The curses of widows and orphans followed it, and will forever follow those who are responsible for it. We have no illustrated papers to multiply and exaggerate the story of these horrors, if they can be exaggerated, and no courts-martial and military commissions to brand with infamous punishment the guilty, but the tale *must be told.* Let the fathers and mothers tell it to their offspring, and bequeath the memory

"As a rich heritage unto their children."

The day will come in this century or the next for History; and—if there is a God, whose wrath is still kindled by brothers' blood—for vengeance.

Tuesday, June 21*st.*—As I expected, the capture of Petersburg was a mere falsehood, which having accomplished its purpose, be the same financial or political, is now shelved as quietly as the same versatile people sacrifice a principle or decapitate a general, when either has served their turn.

When news comes from a great distance or through many hands, these astonishing departures from truth may be accounted for, bat these dispatches were written at City Point, within nine miles of Petersburg, and where their authors must have known they were false.

The further issue of cracker-boxes to the prisoners

was prohibited to-day, so that an elegant arrangement by which I proposed, in company with five or six others, to become a P. L. aristocrat is postponed, if not prevented utterly. As our rulers do not vonchsafe any excuse for this act, which was probably a mere freak, we are of course left to conjecture as to the cause, and guesses at the motives of the conduct of these worthies are not likely to prove signally profitable.

Io triumphe! I received to-day a letter! To ordinary mortal eyes this may seem nothing more than a common quadrangle of MS., distinguished by the *imprimatur* of a certain official outside the "pen," who stamps our correspondence "Prisoner's Letter, Examined," but to me, hungering and thirsting after news of home, this was as grateful as the first golden distillation of the grape to our pluvious progenitor in the earliest autumn after the deluge. (N.B. This simile is copyrighted.) The regulations of all the prisons prohibit prisoners from sending or receiving a longer letter than one page. At Point Lookout the ellipsis which may be supposed to follow the word "page," in the "general order," is filled with the words "of note paper." So that one had to acquire a telegraphic habit of writing, or be content to say little. Some geniuses whose fancies refused this mathematical curb, were in the habit of writing their letters at the usual length, and cutting them off by the page and sending them "by detail," very much as ships are said by Baltimore men to be built "Down East," by the mile, and then cut off to suit purchasers:—while others cultivated a microscopic penmanship, which must be eminently useful to them on their return to Dixie, unless paper falls in the market meanwhile.

Tuesday, June 21st.—On the prison bulletin-board —an institution by which general information is conveyed to prisoners—a list was pasted this morning, containing the names of parties for whom there were boxes or packages to deliver, and to my considerable joy, my name appeared among the rest. These presents to, or purchases by prisoners, are delivered at a door in the south side of the inclosure, which opens through the fence and into an office or store-room, where the packages are received, opened, examined, and all that escapes the regulations (and the *regulators)* turned over to the owners. As before remarked, this performance is conducted on the most ascetic principles as respects clothing, no one being allowed to take any articles of outside wear, from hat to shoes (boots are *mala prohibita),* unless he deposits the corresponding article of his existing stock. It becomes necessary, therefore, if one has any article of apparel, that he is not exactly prepared to turn over to his merciful masters, to find some method of evading the laws. This was not very difficult. All that was necessary, was to buy, or beg, or "flank" a suit of clothes, to surrender which would involve no other sacrifice than that purely emotional one which founds our attachment to certain things, on account of an absurd veneration for antiquity. Accordingly, I beat up quarters for half an hour, till I *accumulated* a suit that would have entitled me to an exalted position among the raggedest vagrants in Naples or Constan tinople. My shoes had to be coaxed to stay on, by an arrangement after the fashion of a surcingle, which strapped them to my feet. My hat only deserved the name from the circumstance that in some mythical era of the past, it was attached to certain other, and *relatively very extensive* portions of organized matter, now, alas long resolved into their original elements,— the combination of which constituted the article in question; though I am free to say, it would have required the anatomical intuition of a Cuvier to have deduced the *castor* from the fragment. It being a warm summer-day, I conceived it would excite no suspicion to appear without a coat, so my only other article of external costume was one which, with great and many misgivings, I venture to enter on the catalogue of pantaloons. Verily, verily, never since the martial ancestors of the gay Parisians invented these indispensable institutions of dress (and I have Gibbon's authority for the assertion, that they *deserve* that credit), did such a travesty on costume disgust the eye of taste. Innocent of buttons, both legs out at the knees, stained by time and less tender agencies out of all approach to its original color, with an enormous quadrilateral carved out of it in a location which indeed could best spare so large a tax, but which modesty forbids me to make more particular reference to, it was only by a diligent and scientific application of pins that I could induce it to preserve even a bifurcate appearance, while the assistance of one hand was necessary to keep the entire compilation from demolition, and the wearer from the miserable fate of Parson Adams, in his celebrated nocturnal encounter in the inn. Long ere this, oh, most comical of costumes, thou hast found appropriate service in the terrifying of crows; or—more noble fate—"the paper-mill hath claimed thee for its own."

Thus caparisoned, however, and assuming an air of such desolation as might be considered appropriate to preserve the *tout ensemble,* I wended my way to the office. As I passed along, my ragamuffin appearance excited, of course, a little comment, which I bore with philanthropic patience till one villanous "reb," presuming on the position of the hand that was doing the duty of a pair of suspenders, suggested, with a solemn wag of his head, "Maybe a little Jamaiky ginger mout help yer, mister!" The charitable motive disarmed any resentment I might have felt at the insult to my appearance.

To the office I went, however, but my preparations turned out to be all in vain. My package consisted of a beef tongue and a can of "solidified cream." I returned to my quarters with my plunder, gave myself a denuding shake, which reduced my dress pretty much to the condition of the memorable "one-horse shay," and summoning my messmates, soon forgot both the troubles and the farce of costuming, in diligent application to the "provant." Oh, Dalgetty, prince and prototype of the military Bohemian, with what wisdom and justice did you assign the highest place in the soldier's scale to "rations!"

It is quite humiliating to those whose idea of the superior dignity of humanity is so very exalted, to confess how much of the good and evil, great and little, objective as well as subjective of life, is dependent on the average dinner a man gets, but the fact is indisputable. I claim no originality for this reflection. Forty years ago Byron wrote—

> ———"all   human   history   attests
> That happiness for man—the hungry sinner—
> Since Eve ate apples, much depends on dinner."

And whoever troubles his brain with the unfashionable labor of thinking, will be apt to conclude with me that much besides happiness hangs on the same thread. What is the reason that the Romans conquered the world? Merely this—they were generous feeders. Who can account for the fact that the hardy Scotsman has not been able to hold his own against his less stalwart neighbor below the Tweed, except as a result of the fact that oatmeal, though flanked by usquebaugh, is no match for wheat flour with only beer for an ally? Why have the Hindoos so steadily and so extensively bowed their necks before the English? Preachers, and philanthropists, and editors, and place-men, all have their ready-made theories to account for the phenomenon; but the patent fact, which they won't confess, because it don't suit their hypotheses, is, that Nana Saib ate *rice,* but Havelock *roast-beef.* Why was Cassius a conspirator? Because he was "lean and hungry." Why did Napoleon lose Waterloo? Merely because he was too fat, or, as some irreverent historian affirms, because he had the stomach-ache, as he confesses. Why won't revolution succeed in Ireland? Depend upon it, the root of the mischief is the potato. Who could be humane on raw beef and Cognac, or virtuous on truffles and Lynnhaven oysters? Caramba! the thing cannot be.

Shakspeare recognized the general connection in his broad assertion, "Fat paunches have lean pates," and many a long century before him, the candid Horace, regardless of the danger he ran of having his criticism turned on his jolly, rotund little self, uttered the same thought—

> "Pingue pecus domino facias, et cetera, *prœter,*
> *Ingenium.*"

Indeed, I am not sure that those philosophers were wholly in the wrong who located the soul in the stomach; and being an optimist, I find great comfort in the thought that if this be true, few will be lost for voluntary want of attention to this tabernacle of the nobler part of man.

CHAPTER X.

Officers moving.—Negro insolence.—Fires out across the dead line.—
Improvising furniture.—Designs on a "nail kag."—Negro regiment to the front.—A new prison at Elmira.—The Fourth of July
in vinculis. —Noble Maryland.

Thursday, June 23 *d.*—The officers who were confined in a pen near us were to-day removed, preparatory to sending them to Fort Delaware. It has been
determined to keep no commissioned prisoners at this
point. To-day the negroes are again on guard, and
are very insolent. Like all the rest of these sable patriots, they seem to have exhausted the resources of
darkness to form their complexions, and their conduct
is as black as their skin. They curse and swear at the
prisoners, level their guns at them, and threaten to
fire, "jis to make de dam rebs scatter;" will not allow a group of three to talk together, and at night
bully and beat every prisoner that they meet. A
whisper in a tent loud enough to be heard by these
patriots is a signal for their entrance, when they steal
what they want, and drown remonstrance in a volley
of oaths, if they are sober; and likely enough, balls, if
they are drunk.

An order was issued to us to-day, prohibiting the
lighting of any more fires in camp; so that the extra
cooking which we have been able to give our half-raw

rations is foreclosed. This order was given, as we were officially informed, to prevent the fouling of the camp which cooking occasioned; but the truth was, as I found to my cost, it was designed to prevent the prisoners from making their food fit to eat.

As the washer*men* were still permitted to boil their clothing on the beach outside the pen, I carried my chips there, and made up a fire to cook the raw meat we were furnished with at the mess-room. An ebony "man and brudder" soon invited me to "put out dat fire, or I'll put you out dam quick;" and convinced me of the propriety of obedience by certain manipulations of his musket which were not agreeable.

The "nig" followed me with his eye, anxious, as I soon found, to pick a quarrel. He was soon gratified on this wise. Little bridges of a couple of planks were placed across the dead-line opposite the gates of the pen, to enable wheelbarrows and other vehicles to pass in and out; but pedestrians could as easily step across the fatal trench, since it was only a few inches wide, and they constantly did so. On this occasion, as a great many were passing out of the camp over the bridge, I stepped across the ditch. I heard some one cry, "Halt!" but, conscious of violating no order, I had no suspicion that the summons was addressed to me, when I was startled by some one crying out, "Take care, he is going to fire!" Turning round out of curiosity, I found my sable friend making preparations for my funeral!

As soon as I faced him, he shouted out with a vulgar oath, "Come across dat line and walk over the bridge, you dam rebel."

5

I of course stepped back across the ditch, and accommodated his sable highness by crossing it on the plank as directed.

So I carried my salt horse and my pot of unboiled water back to my comrades with exceeding disconsolateness.

Before nightfall our Yankee sergeant visited the various tents in our division and "confiscated" the light-wood we had purchased and stored away as fuel. It was a trifling matter, unquestionably, but the air of satisfaction with which this worthy, "clothed in a little brief authority," performed his task, gave to each motion of the vulgarian the sting of a personal affront.

The members of the Fourth division came to exceeding grief to-day. Some of the tin cans in which our slops were furnished were missing from the tables of that division after breakfast, and when the "rebs" of that section marched up for their dinner they were quietly told to expect no rations until the missing cups were found. The Edinburgh Review rose, according to Sydney Smith, by "stress of politics," and I suppose the return of the missing tin-ware may be coerced by stress of starvation. At all events, the Fourth division "rebs" must test the efficacy of the system through much alimentary tribulation.

I find I am becoming sybaritic, and though a crumpled rose-leaf might not interfere fatally with my sleep, the planks on the floor of my kind host's house certainly do. This morning, therefore, I conceived a French bedstead—this evening it is *un fait accompli*. An empty flour-barrel and two poles about six and a

half feet long constituted my stock. I knocked the
barrel to pieces and nailed the staves across the poles,
placed about two feet apart and parallel. Then nail-
ing over all the hoops, which I had straitened out for
the purpose, I had a comfortable, springy bedstead,
which in the daytime I shall place on its end at the
back of the ranche out of the way, and in the night-
time extend at length, between the bunks with which
our house is already supplied. This is the cheapest
and best of improvised bedsteads, and I commend it
to gentlemen of expensive tastes who may be similarly
circumstanced.

The boys are laughing at the summons which S., one
of my fellow Petersburgers, got to-day from a negro
sentinel. S. had on when captured, and I suppose
still possesses, a tall beaver of the antique pattern, considered inseparable from extreme respectability in the
last decade, and for many a year before. While wan-
dering around the inclosure, seeking, I suspect, *"what
he might devour,"* he accidentally stepped beyond
"the dead-line," and was suddenly arrested by a
summons from the nearest negro on the parapet, who
seemed to be in doubt whether so well dressed a man
could be a "reb," and therefore whether he should
be shot at once.

"White man, you b'long in dar?"

"Yes."

"Well, ain't you got no better sense den to cross
dat line?"

"I did not notice the line."

"Well you better notice it, an' dat quick, or I'll
blow half dat *nail kag* off!"

It is needless to say that the owner of the "nail kag" "stood not upon the order of his going."

Friday, July 1*st.*—To-day one of the negro regiments that has been guarding us—the Thirty-sixth United States Colored—left this point for the front, their places being taken by the Fifth Massachusetts Colored Cavalry and another black regiment, ordered here, it is said, by Butler, for cowardice in presence of the enemy (good joke for Butler). Negro-like, the outgoing regiment left singing, in a most orthodox plantation whine, the National (African) Anthem, "John Brown's body lies mouldering in the ground."

One of the disgraced (!) darkies was standing near me as the regiment passed our gates with every jaw extended, and with a knowing wag of the head, he observed, "Niggers is such fools. Dey is gwine away wid der moufs open, but dey'll come back wid 'em shet, I 'speck." On they travelled, making the welkin ring with—

> "John Brown's body lies a-mouldering in the ground,
> John Brown's body lies a-mouldering in the ground,
> John Brown's body lies a-mouldering in the ground,
> But his soul is a-marching on."

All of which, and much more of the same sort, was chanted with that monotonous cadence that many a time and oft we have all heard at camp-meetings and corn-shuckings, under the inspiring influence of religion in the one, and—*horresco referens*—rot-gut in the other. It was not many weeks before their mangled bodies were clogging up that horrible valley of death which the fatal mining of Grant clove in a certain memorable hill-side of Petersburg, where, for nearly an hour, at short grape-range, the cannoneers of the Army of Northern Virginia dealt destruction from their safe embrasures upon the writhing, power-less, and baffled columns of assault.

Saturday, July 2 d.—A notice was posted on the public bulletin-board to-day, requiring all prisoners who were brought from Belle Plain on the 23d of May to fall in at the gate at nine A.M. This is pre-paratory to a move somewhere; and the rumor is that Elmira, New York, a sort of fungus of the Erie Rail-road, is to be the point of destination. I hope our turn will not be long coming, or this infernal water will settle the question of exchange, as far as regards me personally, in a very unsatisfactory manner. I am not at all superstitious in the manner of sepulture, but if I have an antipathy thereanent, it is to being buried at Point Lookout. I hardly think the example of Wellington in the old world, or Webster in the new, both of whom died by the salt water, could reconcile me to such a fate just now.

Monday, July 4th.—This is the day that all America was wont to dedicate to lemonade, ice-cream, picnics, and patriotism. I remember well one "Fourth," so long back that I decline to enter into any vulgar arith-metic about it, when, in obedience to a custom almost as universal as that sanguinary Indian rule which de-nies the privileges of the tribe to a young man until he scalps an enemy, I, who write to you, assumed the *toga virilis* by means of a Fourth of July oration, and worked myself into a perspiration, and my amiable auditory into demonstrative gratification, over the

glories and greatness, the prowess and the perpetuity
of the Union! And here am I, this blessed day of
grace, suffering condign pains and penalties, at the hands
of the successor of Washington, for the—but hang
politics. I made a vow twenty days ago, that unless
mightily moved by some Yankee, I would eschew all
thought of politics until I saw my own good flag once
more; and as you have done me no particular harm
that I wot of, most courteous reader, I'll spare you.
Suffice it to say, that Point Lookout, July 4, 1864,
and Petersburg, July 4, 18—, were about as different
dates, in all their relations to the writer, as any two
points of time could well be. On the latter occasion,
I enjoyed various exhilarations, which now, in the ret-
rospect, refuse to arrange themselves in any regularity
or method, but present a confused melange of ice-
cream, Declaration of Independence, sherry-cobbler,
military procession, national salute, fruit-cake, toasts,
orator of the day, excessively wet shirt-collar, millions
of fans,—I wont *qualify* as to the number,—pretty
women (mainly from the country!) congratulations,
and an immense dinner—admire the climax! But the
other date ushered in divers miseries, and nothing but
hard-tack and fat pork! Verily, verily, Plautus is
right, "The gods have us men for footballs."

> "Enimvero Dii nos, quasi pilas
> Homines habent."

All this, and much more of the same sort, which I
charitably spare you, ran through my mind as I took
my usual morning promenade on the beach to-day,
and watched the streamers and flags spreading from

maintop to bowsprit over the wicked-looking gunboat
that watched (and showed its teeth, for that matter)
like a naval Cerberus over the gates of our "pen."
At twelve M. the Stars and Stripes were flung out,
and the national salute of thirty-I-do not-know-how-
many guns fired, amid the piping and drumming and
braying of "Yankee Doodle," from divers bands
ashore and aboard. The "rebs" had no idea, however, of permitting the Yanks to monopolize the fun;
and on a couple of the patrician mansions of "Cracker-
box Row" there might be seen diminutive copies of
our own Southern Cross, gayly flung out "to the bold
breeze of heaven," after the manner detailed in one
of the many metrical villanies which have been palmed
off on the long-suffering Southern people, under the
name of National Anthems, any time these four years
back.

I noticed particularly on the "Home Again" house
a pretty Confederate flag, which must either have
been manufactured inside or conveyed very surrep-
titiously from the outside by some ingenious sym-
pathizer—a *woman* "for a ducat"—who had the
courage to dare, and the wit to baffle, Yankee jealousy
of every thing suggestive of the hated Confederacy.

This house was occupied by Marylanders; and the
mention of the name suggests to me that I will not
have a better opportunity than this to challenge for
these exiles from that noble State, a reversal of the
unjust reproach which has been cast upon her from
various quarters, and in various forms, in the South.
It is doubtless true, that there are cowards and knaves
in Maryland, and it is not less true, that every South-

ern State and Northern could furnish many a sample
to place by the side of those who have earned so much
reproach for her. But it is quite as true, that no people
in any part of the world have furnished more illustrious
examples of pure, unselfish, uncompromising, all-sacri-
ficing devotion than now distinguishes the citizens of
that gallant State. I knew much of this before. I had
seen her brave sons suffering a long and bitter exile
from all that was dear to them—uncheered by hope
of speedy return—cut off from their families—hurled,
in many cases, from affluence to poverty—condemned
to the disheartening spectacle of witnessing their possessions enjoyed, their friends imprisoned, their State
controlled by an abhorred race, imported from New
England to colonize and *convert* Maryland. And yet,
I had seen them gallantly bearing a banner, which no
hand of ours has been able to maintain on any spot of
Maryland's soil, for thirty days, hoping against hope,
while the weary years rolled on, for the day of deliverance, and faltering not, nor failing, though their
hearts sank in the pain and palsy of that hope forever
deferred. So have I seen her fair daughters, many of
them tenderly and delicately raised, forced to choose
exile as the alternative of a jail—perchance for some
act of common humanity to a Confederate soldier—or
voluntarily embracing the perils and hardships, because in their generous, loyal hearts, approving the
principles and sympathizing with the sufferings of our
beleaguered Confederacy, spending their days near
the hospital cot, and devoting their nights to the toils
of the busy needle, for an army that has never yet
been strong enough to give them an escort for one

short day to their hospitable city of monuments. All this have I seen, and have seen it oftentimes repeated, and I have placed it to the credit of that noble State against the recreancy of the few Marylanders who have skulked among us, and the many *not Marylanders,* who have counterfeited the name to cloak their cowardice. But it was not till I became a prisoner that I appreciated to the full the devotion of her children. When I saw them cheerfully enduring the privations of a long imprisonment, almost within sight of their own homes, many of them persecuted with solicitations from their nearest relatives to come out, take the oath, and enjoy every comfort that wealth and society can offer, all of them conscious that a word would unlock the prison-gates, and send them forth to their families, with no one to question or reproach them; and then learned, that of the many hundreds of Marylanders, at various periods, who were tenants of that pen, some of whom are prisoners of over a year's standing, *not five in all* had taken the oath of allegiance to the Yankee Government, I felt that the best of us might take a lesson from their patriotic constancy. And when, a few months afterwards, I saw some of these very men marched like felons through their own fair city, without permission to whisper a word—scarcely to cast a look at mothers and sisters standing by, who were heart-hungry for the poor privilege of a mere greeting, and yet saw no cheek blanch, no muscle quiver, no weakening of their proud resolve to fight the fight out for principle, through every sacrifice and every peril—calmly, nay, with a smile on their lips, half of triumph, half of scorn, answering the

5*

taunts of their keepers—they marching from prison to
exile, while I was marching from prison to my home—
I felt as I now feel, the wish that the Confederacy was
peopled with such men. Let not their names nor their
deeds die—let some pen, meet for the task, gather now,
while the events are fresh, the memorials of her children in this war for freedom where they have so little
to hope—so much to fear, and though the fortune of
war should separate them and the Confederacy from
their beloved State, let history do justice to the faithful living, and let a nation's gratitude lay immortal
laurels o'er

> "The sacred grave
> Of the last few who, vainly brave,
> Die for the land they cannot save."

A year has elapsed since these sentences were
penned, and every thing has since changed; yet I cannot find it in my heart to alter a line then written. I
hoped then that the deeds of the second "Maryland
Line" might have a fitting historian, and that in the
joy of the birth of a new, nation, they might find a
recompense for the travail they so freely shared.
There is no nation to bless them now, and her daughters sit like Judah's by the waters of Babylon, weeping over the lost hopes of their kindred; and her
sons, proscribed and persecuted, denied the poor privilege, in many cases, of merely living in the noble
State that bore them, are scattered over the land.
Yet the immortal seed of freedom was not in vain
planted there by Baltimore, and Carroil, and Howard,
for while I write, an honored son of that State

famous in statesmanship and in law, is pleading with majestic eloquence in both forums for the preservation of the poor remnant of civil liberty that fanaticism has spared.

CHAPTER XI.

More arrivals.—The sinking of the Alabama.—"Miss Gilbert's Career."—Old Jubal after the Suabians.—A disagreeable order.—Working details.—Changing quarters.

Tuesday, July 5 th.—Another batch of prisoners, those who arrived here on the 8th of June, received a summons yesterday to be in readiness to leave, and were carried out of camp. As we were the next tenants to these in the order of time, I presume we will be next called.

Two items of news are furnished us by the papers to-day—one, the anticipation of a raid by Early into Maryland—the other, the destruction of the "Alabama" by the "Kearsage." Fortunately the two came together, so we managed to endure the latter with some composure, though both surprised and mortified that Semmes should have lost his ship, and the Confederacy his invaluable services, for a time at least, on a point of professional etiquette. Still it may be said of most naval as well as most other duels, that the result is purely an accident. The exploding or failure to explode of a particular shell—an event utterly beyond the skill or control of any one aboard—may, and in this instance did, settle the whole matter. No one suggests a doubt of the courage and coolness with which Semmes pursued his chivalric resolve, and the result might well have been anticipated, aside from the intervention of chance, when we reflect that one vessel was a merchantman in fact, as far as regards its pursuits, with a crew of common sailors with but one battle experience, while the other was a man-of-war with a crew trained especially and exclusively for this description of duty. And yet the Yankees themselves admit that if a certain shell that penetrated their stern had exploded, Messrs. Winslow & Co. would have been very thankful to the "Greyhound" for any such little favors as were subsequently extended to the Confederates; while the French account adds that Captain Semmes endeavored from the first to discard the element of accident from the fight, by getting to close quarters, and settling the question in a fair, stand up, hand to hand encounter—a manœuvrc that the Yank had no stomach for, and successfully used his superior sailing qualities to avoid. Still it is a great victory for Doodledom, and no higher compliment could be paid the "Alabama" and her gallant company, than is furnished in the extravagant joy of our enemies over the loss of the "great pirate." The "old flag" may again perchance steal up to the "top" of the boasted merchant marine, a half a million tons of which the dreaded "pirate" drove from the seas in six months! The hundreds of pious frauds whereby nominal transfers of Boston and New York bottoms were made to English and French owners, so that the "Yanks" might pocket the receipts without taking the risks of the carrying trade, will now be repented of and renounced—said frauds being no longer profitable. Commodore Vanderbilt may make the run from Panama without a convoy, and Cape Cod may fish in peace.

Selah!

Meanwhile the Suabians in the Quaker State are hurrying off their beeves and blinding their horses,* and General Wallace is putting Baltimore in a state of defence,—an operation that seems "always doing, never done."

I have been suffering for some days past for something to read, and to day, by accident, stumbled over a very fresh-looking volume in one of the cook-houses, entitled "Miss Gilbert's Career,"—brilliant in all the gorgeousness of clear print and faultless binding.

The title-page announces that it was the twentieth thousand, a circumstance I can only explain, in common justice to Yankee taste, by supposing that the twentieth thousand was printed before the first ditto. Such a common-place vulgarity as Miss Gilbert, I undertake to say, never could have been produced on any soil of earth other than "Massachusetts Bay and Providence Plantations." There are situations, however, wherein any thing in print is endurable, and I waded, with the patience of a professional proof-

---

* This perfectly original barbarity was committed time and again on the occasion of General Lee's entry into Pennsylvania, in June, 1863. Rather than take the trouble to remove their horses, they would blind the poor brutes by puncturing their eyes with a needle, thus making them useless to us for army purposes, while their value as draft animals, or for farm uses was not very largely impaired. In many cases we found the poor beasts with their eyes still overflowing with tears and blood, from the merciless hands of their masters.

reader, through every sentence and syllable of the dreary platitudes of Miss Gilbert! I record this incident solely as a contribution to the next edition of Abercrombie on the Mind, since it establishes beyond cavil the enormous *vis inertiœ* of the human intellect; and I commend the book to all those who believe that the brain, like the muscles, can be strengthened by subjection to unusual and repeated strains. Dr. Winship, the modern Hercules, boasted that he could raise three thousand six hundred pounds—a capacity he acquired by constant effort in that direction, and I have no doubt that equal diligence in the mental line would insure results equally marvellous. If any one wishes to try the experiment, I recommend mental calisthenics with a pair of such books as the aforesaid "Career," as I consider it about as heavy as the stout doctor's dumb-bells (the source of all his marvellous strength), which weighed as much as a flour-barrel apiece!

Wednesday, July 6th.—More rumors. Grant, say the correspondents, has demanded the surrender of Petersburg. *Peut-être!* Early is playing the wild with the Baltimore and Ohio Railroad, and, greatest grief of all *to us,* the sutler informs us that the further sale of articles of luxury and food to us will be suspended, as the authorities are informed that our sutlers are prohibited from selling, such things to their prisoners. As to the luxuries, the inhibition in Dixie is not likely. The sutler who could contrive to get such an article as an orange or a box of Mason's blacking, would deserve burning at the stake, being conclusively guilty of dealing with the devil. As to necessaries, the government of the Confederacy would be very glad if the sutlers would take the Commissary Department entirely off their hands. My old friend, Colonel Northrup,* is terribly exercised on the subject I *know*.

But the reason of the order is of no consequence to us, it is the order which troubles us. On hearing the announcement, I made my moan to the first acquaintance I met, who happened to be an old prisoner. He greatly calmed my fears by assuring me that this was an old dodge in the pen, designed *to bring in rapidly*

---

* I cannot let slip the occasion of paying the tribute of my admiration to the most incorruptible integrity and a capacity of no mean order displayed in the administration of the Commissary Department of the Confederate States, under Colonel Northrup. From the beginning of the war, the labors of his office were great, and its responsibilities most onerous. Before it concluded, both became simply stupendous; and although Mr. Davis, yielding to a popular clamor which he did not feel himself warranted in resisting, substituted him in the fourth year of the war by another gentleman, the experiment did not meet expectations, for the plain reason that there *are* things impossible to man. I had not met Colonel N. for some time, when on the evening of the 1st of July, 1865, having been committed to Castle Thunder, Richmond, by General Alfred Howe Terry, for the crime of calling Clement C. Clay a gentleman, and refusing that compliment to Major-General Hunter and his associates on the Military Commission, I was somewhat surprised to see Colonel N. marched into the jail under guard. He had been arrested, he never knew for what, and was kept among drunkards, rowdies, and felons for some months, when he was thrust out of prison, as he had been thrust in—without a reason.

"Hail Columbia! Happy land, etc."

the sutler's checks in order to the entire disposal of the stock on hand, which was probably larger than he desired to keep this hot weather. This was very reassuring, as I had just received notice that there was a "money letter" in the major's hands for me, whose advent and use I anticipated with much watering of the mouth.

The ruse of course succeeded, and the sutler's "powerful" butter, game herrings, animated cheese, and sour meal began to disappear with a celerity that must have been very satisfactory to him, if not to the deluded Confederates, who were thus seduced into an unusual quantity of purchases.

Thursday, July 7th.—The supply of water is getting very scant, and the quality very infamous. Guards have been placed over some of the pumps to prevent waste, and these being "negroes," it is necessary, in order to get a drop, to ask permission in respectful terms of the sable sentinels, who, to do them justice, do not seem disposed to abuse their position. I attribute this to the circumstance that these are negroes who have been in service; and any soldier will tell you that an active campaign inspires very humane sentiments towards soldiers. With every precaution, the amount is still so insufficient that a water-boat had to be sent down from Baltimore to-day to furnish a supply to the hospitals; and a detail has been engaged most of the morning wheeling in barrels of it for the use of the sick.

There is quite a contention for the privilege of working in this, as on other details, there being some privileges attached thereto. Almost every day there

is some description of labor to be performed outside
of the pen, for which volunteers are sought and easily
obtained among the prisoners. Those selected for
the work are mustered into a company, their names
taken down, and under Yankee guards they are
carried outside to the scene of their work. This
consists principally in the unloading of vessels at the
wharf, in building hospitals, commissary store-rooms,
stables, etc., etc. The legitimate benefits of these
details are: first, occupation; second, a little liberty;
third, the chance to hear some news; and fourth, a
small piece of tobacco. The semi-legitimate benefits
are: the gathering up of refuse pieces of plank, old iron,
nails, and the like, which command a high price (in
tobacco or hard-tack) within the "pen." The ille-
gitimate, and I fear the most operative inducement
with some of the unregenerate "rebs," is the opportunity of pilfering along the wharf and among the
vessels whose cargoes they are discharging, which the
nature of their duties frequently affords. From one
cause or another—generally, I suppose, from a combination of several—the detail list is always full, and
places thereon command a premium.

In the earlier period of Point Lookout history,
there was an additional advantage in these details, inasmuch as the opportunity of escape was thereby frequently afforded and embraced, but the multiplication
of the precautions which experience of "rebel" ingenuity occasioned, has rendered the blockade for
several months past pretty effectual.

Friday, July 8 th.—No newspapers permitted to be
brought into camp to-day. Early is doubtless fright

ening Father Abe prodigiously, and he fears the stimulating effect on his misguided enemies in prison. The weather has been furiously hot for a week past, and as the earth is a sparkling sand, and every thing about us is a glaring white, many, besides myself, are suffering with inflamed eyes,—a chronic disorder here.

Saturday, July 9th.—To-day is the first mensiversary of my imprisonment. Any super-fastidious reader who objects to my word-coinage, is hereby informed that he is at perfect liberty to draw his pencil through the obnoxious polysyllable and substitute therefor any word, or form of words, that will better please him, but I hold it, nevertheless, to be a perfectly defensible creation.

Our rations grow daily worse—the soup more watery, the pork fatter and more rancid, the beef leaner and more stringy; and the poor devils who have no "sutler's checks" hanker after the loyal flesh-pots.

Another month here and I shall become a candidate for one of the piled-up pine-boxes that flanked us on the left as we entered the pen, grimly suggestive of the fate so singularly bewailed in Ecclesiastes, "dying without a burial," or any thing deserving the name of one.

Hooray! which is Irish for evoe! and incomparably better. Hooray, Company B, Thirteenth Division, among others is summoned to the gate, and as I had the fortune to be transferred to that squad a few days ago, I pack my diminutive wallet, glad to leave this hole, though for Spitzbergen. We were marched to the provost-marshal's office, counted and listed, and turned into the "Officer's pen," where we were kept until

our muster-rolls were made out. Here we were permitted to change our "checks" into greenbacks, and
in the midst of this interesting piece of financiering
our former hero of the grape-vine cane and mutton-
chop whiskers appeared at the gate, and ordered us
to "fall in."

Between one and two o'clock, two hundred and
eighty-two of us were marched to the wharf and put
aboard a narrow log of a propeller, rejoicing in the
sounding title "El Cid."

Down a crazy ladder into a reeking hold, where the
heat and stench would have overpowered any other
animal than a Confederate prisoner, we trooped along,
packing ourselves away in the fashion which the
mellifluous Wilberforce was so fond of expatiating on,
under the name of "the horrors of the middle passage," until the last "Southern Confederate" crossed
the taffrail, the gang-plank was drawn in, and at two
P. M. we turned our backs on Point Lookout, we
hoped forever,

"O wer weis, etc.,"—you'll find the rest in Schiller's
Don Carlos; but lest the great German play may not
be at hand, I recall a good, if free, translation in
Robby Burns' proverb,

> "The best laid schemes of mice an' men
> Aft gang agley."

CHAPTER XII.

Deliverance against sea-going.—A disgusting trip.—A friend in need.—Nectar.—New York harbor.—On the Erie Railroad.—Sympathizers.—At Elmira.—El Cid anathematized.

THE man who first invented going to sea was an infidel and a fool, a misanthrope, and probably a marauder, a supereminent donkey and a filibuster, *hostis humani generis,* and should have been outlawed accordingly. The element is proverbially treacherous, the dangers are great, the inconveniences infinite, the results moonshine, and, to crown all, beneficent Nature has implanted in every human stomach an instinctive and vigorous protest against the practice, which ought to satisfy any reasonable being that it never was designed that a creature innocent of fins, tail, or a shell, should go out of sight of land. I admit that the whale-oil supply was for a long time an obstacle to the general acceptance of my view of the case, but the vast fields of petroleum recently discovered knock the wind out of that argument, and allow me to indulge the reasonable hope that if Pit Hole holds out, and Oil Creek does not suffer from a drought, I shall one day have the satisfaction of participating in a general auction of all marine properties,"on account of whom it may concern."

The fact is, there is nothing redeeming about the infernal sea-going system. You get up in the morning, and there is no newspaper; you stroll out to settle your bitters, and a dozen paces in any direction will introduce you to a shark; you stagger in to breakfast, and the coffee slides into your beefsteak, and both into your lap; you get up, and in ten minutes you discover, in the language of the luckless Yellow-plush, "Wot tin basins was made for;" the day passes, and there is no post-office, no business, no counting-room, no children run over, no street cries, no omnibus, no dog-fight, no civilization: it snows, and you can't go sleighing; it is fair, and you can't take a drive; it rains, and you can't roll tenpins, or get satisfactorily drunk; pale spectres with pendent jaws and watery eyes, all by a strange centrifugal force flying towards the outside of the ship, pass you at every instant; and after a day dismally dragged through in every conceivable discomfort, you turn in at night to a closet not large enough to swing a cat in, and tumble into a berth which looks so much like a coffin, that you dream, before you are well asleep, of attending your own funeral!

So your days creep along, if you have vitality enough to survive, destitute of fox-hunts or flirtations, law or literature, politics or opera, fashion-plates or scandal, telegrams or taxes; and if the old scythe-bearer comes to your relief, you are sewed up in a sack with a thirty-two pound shot at your heels, and tossed to the fishes as remorselessly as the beef bones from yesterday's soup!

Gonzalo was a very Solomon. Hear him:

"Now would I give a thousand furlongs of sea for an acre of barren ground: long heath, brown furze, any thing. The wills above be done, but I would fain die a dry death."

All these objections are valid, if you are a first-class passenger aboard a first-class steamer. "Phancy our feelinx," then, when you remember that we were packed like sheep on a cattle-train, in the hold of a villanous tub, in the middle of July, with no ventilation, except what was afforded by two narrow hatchways (there being no side-lights), and permission to put our heads above the deck being only accorded to two at a time, and then for five minutes, so that it required one hundred and fifty times five minutes, or over half the day, to elapse before you could get your second gasp of fresh air! And then our ship was such a crazy and unseaworthy craft, that in the event of a storm there was little prospect of our ever seeing land again, except on the consoling hypothesis of Pisanio, that

"*Fortune* brings in some boats that are not steered."

In this delightful situation, the sun melting the pitch in the seams over our heads, and not air enough stirring to raise a ripple, we stretched ourselves on the lower deck in a desperate state of disgust, with only energy enough to pray for a short passage or a heavy gale,—blessings craved in vain. Many of us were seasick, all were hungry, and there was a unanimous devotion of all Yankeedom to the devil. During the night I stole aloft once, but was ordered down by a sentinel with the manners of a hog and the accent of a New England clock-pedler.

Any thing short of a wheelbarrow ought to make the run from Point Lookout to New York (our destination) in thirty hours, or thirty-five at the most; it took us just forty-six, although the sea was as calm as a river, nothing breaking the smoothness of its treacherous surface, except that infernal stomach-pump, known as the "ground-swell,"—a submarine wave which constantly beats from the shore, and was intended by beneficent Nature to prevent her children from the folly of navigation, by circling the whole ocean with this (unheeded) warning against leaving land.

Sunday, the 10th, was a brilliant day. I took my five-minutes' ration of the deck at sunrise this morning. How the calm, superb majesty of such a scene, the golden god scattering his largesse of rubies over the great deep, crowning each wavelet with a gem; the swelling ocean broken by no ruffling storm, but surging with long unbounded waves to the very gates of the morning; a sky warm and glorious with the purple flush and splendor of the full dawn,—how such a scene, in its beauty, grandness, immensity, tranquillity, contrasts with and rebukes the petty blustering and passions and paltry ambitions of men! How their vanities, envies, prides, wranglings, worldliness, stand abashed in the serene presence of these august emblems of the Eternal—Sun and Sea and Sky!

From ten A. M., Saturday the 9th, until we arrived in New York harbor, a period of over fifty hours, our only food was one ration of bread and a couple of ounces of adipose; and what with this and a slight dose of sea-sickness, I was consummately miserable by the time we got into "the Narrows," early Monday morning. I stole up on deck, and hunting up the officer commanding the guard, asked permission to purchase a cup of coffee from the cook, and leave also to remain on deck till I could drink it. He assented readily; and having made the contract with the presiding genius of the galley, I took my seat on a "bit" forward, and drank my fill of the beautiful scene around me.

As we got well up in the channel a little boat rowed off from shore to us, we stopping the while, and with about ten seconds of conversation to the captain, its tenant rowed back with a fee in his pocket. He was the incumbent of the most lucrative office probably in America—the New York Health officer. The screw revolves, and again we are off.

Those who have entered New York harbor by this channel—and what Southron has not, in those days when Gotham was our Ostium and Piræus?—will remember the richness and luxury of the Jersey coast for thirty miles below the city. The land is high, handsomely wooded, and almost every summit is crowned with a stylish country villa—the urban residences of the princes of Wall-street and Broadway;—while in every reach of shore where a surf breaks, a handsome hotel fronts the sea, and rows of piquant little cottages dot the hill-slopes to their tops. As you approach the city, these evidences of wealth and taste increase in number and in magnificence; and you are ushered into the teeming port of the American Venice through a highway of palaces, with here and there a powerful fortress interspersed, to give security to all this rural luxury and elegance.

6

I was musing on all this, indulging my taste for the beautiful, but amazingly hungry and uncomfortable withal, when a Yankee corporal, a German Jew, named Bernstein, as I afterwards learned, came to where I sat, with a smoking cup of coffee in his hand, his own ration for breakfast, and with a courteous apology for having nothing better to offer, insisted on my drinking it. It was idle to tell him that I had engaged to get some from the cook, for he replied, that the cook might not have it to give me, and on my objectting that he would lose his own breakfast, he assured me that he could get another cup, and would be offended if I did not take it. So I accepted it very gratefully. Not all the sherbets that ever Persian poets sung; not Byron's memorable thimble-full of essence frozen out of a bottle of champagne; not "Lachryma Christi," beloved of Sue; not Perkins' "best pale" to a Briton; nor Swartz's imperial "lager" to a Bavarian; nor poteen to a Wexford man; nor usquebaugh to a Highlander; nor train-oil to a Laplander; nor spermaceti candles to the late Czar, could have matched in refreshment that pint of black coffee to me; so true it is that our joys and griefs in this world are nothing after all but questions of arithmetical proportion.

There is no likelihood that these lines will ever meet his eye, but I could wish that such might be their fate, that my friend Bernstein might see that his little act of kindness is not, and will not be forgotten. Before I had finished, he hunted up his haversack, and laid before me as many "hard-tacks" as I could eat, so that when, half an hour afterwards, the cook told

me he had a breakfast for me, I was able to administer alimentary consolation to a couple of hungry
"rebs" below.

It was near midday when we hauled up the channel just off and below the Jersey City end of the lower
ferry to New York; and there we lay till the train on
the Erie Railroad, whose eastern terminus is here, was
ready. I am quite familiar with New York harbor,
and many a spire of the city was as easily recognized
as that of my Virginia home. Every thing seemed as
busy, as "alive," as stirring, as in the same month,
four years before, when I last saw the gay city. The
war was apparently little felt here. The docks were
as crowded; the same unvarying hum filled the sultry
air; the ferry-boats passed with the same surcharged
loads; the wharves were crowded with the same
rushing hordes of porters, hackmen, stevedores, news-
boys, and thieves; and I doubt not, Broadway echoed
to the same endless tide of wheel and foot, and Wall-
street choked its crooked throat with as excited and
thronging a congregation as have ever "bulled and
beared" it in the shadow of old Trinity, on any July
day this quarter of a century past. In the face of all
this wealth, development, material power—all these
vast appliances of conquest—I felt a new pride in our
beleaguered Confederacy, which has had nothing to
oppose to this unexampled affluence of resource except
the unconquerable gallantry of her children, and yet
has fought this fight against such odds as have never
yet stood in the way of freedom, with a calm confidence in the cause, a noble acceptance of sacrifice, an
undaunted courage, a patient hope, a chivalric devo-

tion, that fearlessly challenge the comparisons of history.

While I am indulging in these moralizings, a little boat is shooting out from shore, and in a moment more an officer boards us,. who probably brings news that the train is now waiting, for our "tub" is now turned towards the dock. We are soon alongside, an officer stands at the hatchway to count us as we come up, lest some may conceal themselves in the ship. The count seems satisfactory (yet it was not, for two born idiots remained aboard), we are marched into the depot, a few paces off, and put aboard a train of box and passenger cars, standing ready for us.

Our advent is unexpected, or the Jerseyans are not as curious as their compatriots elsewhere, for there is but a small crowd of spectators, and these gaze on us with a stolid air, which may mean sympathy; probably, however, indifference. By half-past one all was in readiness, the locomotive gave that preliminary shriek, which, according to Sydney Smith, is most like the scream an attorney may be expected to give when the devil gets hold of him, and off we started for Elmira.

The Erie Railroad, as I presume every one *used* to know, runs through the northern counties of New Jersey, and the southern counties of Central and Western New York. It passes through some handsome towns and cities; but the country is considered far inferior to that which lines the Central road. At almost every station we made a lengthy halt, to give way to some regular train passing up or down, and, wherever we stopped, we were the subjects of very

great, and, generally, respectful interest. The guards
rigidly excluded the people from all intercourse with
us, and forbade, under various sanguinary threats, any
assistance being tendered us; still they found it impossible to guard every avenue of approach, and many
a piece of tobacco, package of crackers, and the like,
was handed us by the good people on the route.
The gentler sex was conspicuous in these charities,
and more than once surprised us by furtive exhibi-
tions of little Confederate flags which they had con-
cealed about their persons. At Port Jervis, there
seemed to be a fair prospect of a difficulty between
our guards and the citizens, many of whom persisted,
despite all orders, in making such contributions to our
wants as accidentally lay in their power. Of course,
these agreeable incidents were occasionally diversified by the insults of some sleek non-combatant, whose
valiant soul found congenial occupation in fearful
threats of our indiscriminate massacre, if he could only
lay hands on us. These gentry were, in the main, of
that physical and sartorial type which we always as-
sociate with the idea of extreme orthodoxy—your
sanctimonious, high-seat-in-the-synagogue worthies,
who

> "Compound for sins they are inclined to,
>   By damning those they have no mind to;"

and from the serene heights of their sublime self-con-
ceit, hurl worse anathemas than that *prolix* profanity
of Bishop Ernulphus, at the forlorn publicans below.
You know the canting breed, good reader mine,
wherever you see them; and at home or abroad, in

pulpit or tribune, in Church or State, they everywhere exhibit the same harmonious blending of Heap's hypocrisy with the villany of Carker. Of these lovely lambs, Butler is the god and Kalloch the prophet. He would be a most unreasonable "reb" who would look for any thing but a snarl from these curs.

And thus, amid friends and foes, through gorges and around bluffs, now skimming gayly along a level meadow, and anon "wiring in and wiring out," apparently in the absurd effort to avoid crossing the Susquehannah—a stream so crooked that the engineers who built the road seem to have fancied that, by following up one bank, they would, sooner or later, find themselves on the other—on we steamed till about eight o'clock, Tuesday morning, when we pulled up in the pretty little city of Elmira, which, albeit only about twenty years old, as I hear, contains twelve thousand inhabitants, and is situated on the left bank of the Chemung, a tributary of the Susquehannah. Although at the door of prison, we realized a comparative comfort by contrasting our condition with what it was aboard the "El Cid." This being the last time I shall have occasion to mention this miraculous sample of naval architecture, I here deliberately devote it to the infernal gods, with as honest an unction as ever filled the bosom of the most patriotic Moor, in the times of its great namesake— a gentleman who must have served Moorish mothers with impracticable cherubs a good turn, he frightened the grown ones so prodigiously, according to the authentic histories of Bob Southey, and that unfor-

tunate victim of a liver complaint and an uncongenial
spouse, Mrs. Hemans.*

---

* Bad weeds grow apace, and the Cid illustrated the philosophy if not the letter of the axiom; for the abomination is at
this moment in the harbor of Newbern, N. C., and advertises
for freight and passengers with as much audacity as if it was
a fit craft to carry a load of Brazilian hides.

CHAPTER XIII.

Statistics of Elmira Pen.—The officers.—Samples of Federal cruelty.
—Number of prisoners.—Barrack accommodations.

I PLAINLY foresee that this chapter is going to run
into statistics, and as I have had a reasonable horror
of mathematics from the blessed days when every application of my mind to figures was followed by the
application to my shoulders of something else, I will be
excused for invoking the patience of the reader, assuring him—a favorite lie with flagellatory parents while
"horsing" their heirs—that the pain I inflict causes
me more suffering than it can possibly occasion him.

For more than a year before our arrival, Elmira was
the site of the rendezvous for the drafted men of Western New York. Here the gushing patriots were received and housed, trained to turn out their toes and
survive "hard-tack," and otherwise qualified to patch
the rents in a certain lacerated Anaconda, which has
been prowling around the cotton and tobacco country
with varying fortunes these four years back. These
gay volunteers required three camps, which were sever-
ally denominated "barracks, one, two, and three," and
here they were kept till they graduated in the manual
of arms, and squandered their bounty-money, when
they were incontinently bundled off to the front, a
performance which, according to most authentic aver-

ments, resulted in the absconding of about twenty-five per cent. of the patriots before they ever came in sight of a camp sample of "the old flag."

Now it came to pass, that Mr. Stanton began to feel some apprehension that the "secesh" were getting too numerous at Point Lookout, and offered too tempting a prize to the profane general then menacing the sourkrout and smear-case (?) of the honest Deutschers in rural Pennsylvania, so he ordained and established by imperial ukase a prison in the hyperborean regions of New York, where for at least four months of every year, any thing short of a polar-bear would find locomotion impracticable, and where, therefore, no apprehension need be felt of trouble within, or assault without, for the same interval. Early in July, therefore, the "Yanks" were ousted from Barracks No. 3, and preparations made for receiving the first instalment of prisoners, who arrived on the 6th of July, numbering three hundred and ninety-nine, the four hundredth man having escaped on the way. (The four hundredth man always *will* escape.) On the 11th, two hundred and forty-nine arrived, and the next day *we* were added to the list.

We were escorted to the "pen," by a large concourse of admiring citizens, a number of whom were of the gentler sex, in every stage of development, curiosity being, *in Elmira, a* failing of the sex. A march of about a mile brought us to our prison. We filed in, were counted, divided into companies of a hundred, the roll called, and we were led off to our quarters. These consisted of wooden buildings, about one hundred feet long, by sixteen in width, and high

6*

enough for two rows of bunks. There were about thirty-five of these buildings in the inclosure, standing side by side, in a line parallel to the front of the pen, and about midway the ground. I soon asserted a pre-emption claim to a top bunk in No. 21, the quarter of most of my Petersburg friends, and having deposited my very modest "pack," started out to view my premises.

I found a level plain of about thirty acres of land, situated, as I have said, a mile or so west of Elmira, and immediately on the bank of the Chemung. The ground is unequally divided by a long narrow lake or lagoon, which runs parallel to the river, into two sections, the one furthest from the entrance gate being denominated the Trans-Mississippi Department, in the vernacular of camp. This lake starts within twenty feet of the fence on one side of the pen, and flows under the opposite fence, and the ground beyond the lake is a sandy bottom, indicating what I found, on inquiry, to be the case, that the unruly Chemung occasionally gets uproarious, overflows its banks, and floods the adjacent grounds.

The whole site is a basin surrounded by hills which rise several hundred feet, and are covered richly and thickly with the luxurious foliage of the hemlock, ash, poplar, and pine. This was the most grateful relief from our Point Lookout experience, where nothing met the eye, in any direction, except the sky, water, and prison fence. But a more available and practical improvement was in the water, which was here pure, cool, and abundant, and the new-comers luxuriated in the delicious beverage with the gusto of a lost travel-ler in Sahara, or a repentant legislator after a nocturnal spree.

In the general arrangement of the guard detail there was little difference from Point Lookout, except in the *absence* of the colored guards, and in the *presence* of the officers, all of whom spent a portion of each day within the "pen." A row of tents running parallel with the front fence of the "pen" was assigned to these gentlemen, and until the approach of winter drove them into certain barracks outside, where ventilating arrangements were not so extensive, they continued to occupy them.

Back of the thirty-four or thirty-five barracks, already referred to, is a row of wooden buildings, containing the adjutant's office, dispensary, various rooms of Yankee sergeants, store-rooms, and the like, and back again of these, the mess-rooms and cook-houses, which extend to the lagoon. These, with one or two other buildings, constituted all the appliances of the prison at that time, nor was any change made until the miasma from the lagoon sowed the seeds of febrile disease so widely, that eight or ten hospitals had to be built, and the advent of prisoners by the thousand exhausted the sleeping capacity of the barracks.

The government of this prison was in the hands of Major Henry V. Colt, One Hundred and Fourth New York Volunteers, a gentleman, fair and fat, of not quite forty, five and a half feet high, with a florid complexion, a comfortable *embonpoint,* a very prepossessing appearance and manner, a jaunty way of cooking his hat on the side of his head, and a chronic

attack of smoking cigars, which he invariably holds
in his mouth at about the angle at which mortars are
ordinarily fired.

I perform a very grateful duty, in here bearing testimony to the various admirable qualities of this gentleman, as an officer and a man. Uniformly urbane
and courteous in his demeanor, he discharged the varied, and oftentimes annoying, offices of his post with
a degree of justice to his position and to the men under his charge, a patience, fidelity, and humanity, that
could not be surpassed, and, I fancy, were seldom
equalled, either side of the line, in similar positions.
There was none of the slipshod indifference of Point
Lookout *régime*. Major Colt either discharged in
person or superintended the execution of every duty
respecting the prison, which appropriately claimed his
attention, doing all with the thoroughness of a trained
man of business; and although charged with duties
whose performance demanded almost every moment
of his time, he was always ready to hear and redress
any just complaints that were made to him, if they
were of a character that justified him in interfering,
or that he had the power to remedy, and to afford any
information or assistance, consistently with his position, to the humblest prisoner. It is a pleasant office
to do this justice to an enemy, and to record this off-
set to the many cruelties which are charged, no doubt
justly, to other officers in charge of our unfortunate
prisoners.

The major's adjutant was Captain C. C. Barton, an
active, smart, and rather consequential young gentleman, as adjutants are wont to be — and here I call at-

tention to the fact that these officers constitute a class, *sui generis*, in every army;—but, upon the whole, Barton was a good fellow, notwithstanding he considered Abe Lincoln a Chesterfield, and accounted Grant a compound, in about equal proportions, of King Solomon and Alexander the Great. Captain B. was assisted by a young sergeant, H., who was promoted to an adjutant's place shortly after our arrival, but did not exchange his comfortable quarters for "the front" till the summer was over; and a youth, Frank E., who, in a fit, of spasmodic patriotism, joined a heavy artillery company, before he was out of his teens, and straightway perilled his invaluable life for his beloved country, as an adjutant's clerk, in the dangerous "Department of the Chemung."

In the executive duties of his office, Major Colt was assisted by fifteen or twenty officers, and as many non-commissioned officers, chiefly of the militia or the veteran reserves. Among them were some characters which are worth a paragraph.

There was a long-nosed, long-faced, long-jawed, long-bearded, long-bodied, long-legged, endless-footed, and long-skirted curiosity, yclept Captain Peck, ostensibly engaged in taking charge of certain companies of "rebs," but really employed in turning a penny by huckstering the various products of prisoners' skill—an occupation very profitable to Peck, but generally unsatisfactory, in a pecuniary way, to the "rebs." Many of them have told me of the impossibility of getting their just dues from the prying, round-shouldered captain, who had a snarl and an oath for every one out of whom he was not, at that instant, making money.

Another rarity of the pen was Lieutenant John McC., a braw chiel frae the land o' cakes, who was a queer compound of good-nature and brutality. To some of us he was uniformly polite, but he had his pistol out on any occasion when dealing with the majority of the "Johnnies," and would fly into a passion over the merest nothing, that would have been exceedingly amusing, but for a wicked habit he had of laying about him with a stick, a tent pole— any thing that fell into his hands. He was opening a trench one day, through the camp, when, for the crime of stepping across it, he forced a poor, sick boy, who was on his way to the dispensary for medicine, to leap backwards and forwards over it till he fell from exhaustion amid the voluble oaths of the valiant, lieutenant. One Lieutenant R. kept McC. in countenance by following closely his example. He is a little compound of fice and weasel, and having charge of the cleaning up of the camp, has abundant opportunities to bully and insult, but being, fortunately, very far short of grenadier size, he does not use his boot or fist as freely as his great exemplar. No one, however, was safe from either of them, who, however accidentally and innocently, fell in their way, physically or metaphorically.

Of the same block Captain Bowden was a chip: a fair-haired, light-moustached, Saxon-faced "Yank"— far the worst type of man, let me tell you, yet discovered—whose whole intercourse with the prisoners was the essence of brutality. An illustration will paint him more thoroughly than a philippic. A prisoner named Hale, belonging to the old Stonewall brigade, was discovered one day rather less sober than was allowable to any but the loyal, and Bowden being officer of the guard, arrested him and demanded where he got his liquor. This he refused to tell, as it would compromise others, and any one but a Yankee would have put him in the guard-house, compelled him to wear a barrel shirt, or inflicted some punishment *proportionate to his offence.* All this would have been very natural, but not Bowdenish, so this valorous Parolles determined to apply the torture to force a confession! Hale was accordingly tied up by the thumbs—that is, his thumbs were fastened securely together behind his back, and a rope being attached to the cord uniting them, it was passed over a cross bar over his head and hauled down, until it raised the sufferer so nearly off the ground that the entire weight of his body was sustained by his thumbs, strained in an unnatural position, his toes merely touching the ground. The torture of this at the wrists and shoulder joints is exquisite, but Hale persisted in refusing to peach, and called on his fellow-prisoners, many of whom were witnesses of this refined villany, to remember this when they get home. Bowden grew exasperated at his victim's fortitude, and determined to gag him. This he essayed to accomplish by fastening a heavy oak tent-pin in his mouth; and when he would not open his mouth sufficiently—not an easy operation—he struck him in the face with the oaken billet, a blow which broke several of his teeth and covered his mouth with blood!

On the other hand, some of the officers were as humane and merciful as these wretches were brutal and cowardly, and all who were my fellow-prisoners will recall, with grateful remembrance, Captain Benjamin Munger, Lieutenant Dalgleish, Sergeant-Major Rudd, Lieutenant McKee, Lieutenant Haverty, commissary of one of the regiments guarding us, a whole-souled Fenian, formerly in the book-business in New York, and still there probably, and one or two others.

These officers were assigned in the proportion of one to every company at first, but to every three hundred or four hundred men afterwards, and were charged with the duty of superintending roll-calls, inspecting quarters, and seeing that the men under their charge got their rations; and *the system* was excellent.

During the month of July, four thousand three hundred and twenty-three prisoners were entered on the records of Elmira prison, and by the 29th of August, the date of the last arrivals, nine thousand six hundred and seven.

The barrack accommodations did not suffice for quite half of them, and the remainder were provided with "A" tents, in which they continued to be housed when I left the prison in the middle of the following October, although the weather was piercingly cold. Thinly clad as they came from a summer's campaign, many of them without blankets, and without even a handful of straw between them and the frozen earth, it will surprise no one that the suffering, even at that early day, was considerable.

As I left, however, the contributions of the Confederate Government, which, despairing of procuring an exchange, was taxing its exhausted energies to aid the prisoners, began to come in.

An agent was in New York selling cotton for the purpose, and many boxes of blankets and coarse clothing were furnished from the proceeds of the sale.

This tender regard was a happy contrast to the barbarity of Washington management, which seemed to feel the utmost, indifference to the sufferings of its soldiers, and embarrassed their exchange by every device of delay and every suggestion of stubbornness.

CHAPTER XIV.

Matters medical.—Sanger the sanguinary.—Rebel doctors.—Cruel neglect of the sick.—Deaths at Elmira and Andersonville contrasted.—The Commissary Department.—Punishments.

As I have spoken of the military government of Elmira prison, it may not be inappropriate to pursue the statistical view, now that I am in it, by a brief chapter on the Medical and Commissary Departments, before I resume the thread of the more personal portion of my narrative.

The chief of the former department was a club-footed little gentleman, with an abnormal head and a snaky look in his eyes, named Major E. L. Sanger. On our arrival in Elmira, another surgeon, remarkable chiefly for his unaffected simplicity and virgin ignorance of every thing appertaining to medicine, played doctor there. But as the prisoners increased in numbers, a more formal and formidable staff was organized, with Sanger at the head.

Sanger was simply a brute, as we found when we learned the whole truth about him *from his own people*. If he had not avoided a court-martial by resigning his position, it is likely that even a military commission would have found it impossible to screen his brutality to the sick, although the fact that the United States hanged no one for the massacre of Indian women and sucking infants during the year 1865, inspires the fear that this systematic * * * * * * * * of Confederate prisoners would have been commended for his patriotism.

He was assisted by Dr. Rider, of Rochester, one of the few "copperheads" whom I met in any office, great or small, at the North. My association was rather more intimate with him than with any of the others, and I believe him to have been a competent and faithful officer. Personally, I acknowledge his many kindnesses with gratitude. The rest of the "meds" were, in truth, a motley crew in the main, most of them being selected from the impossibility, it would seem, of doing any thing else with them. I remember one of the worthies, whose miraculous length of leg and neck suggested "crane" to all observers, whose innocence of medicine was quite refreshing. On being sent for to prescribe for a prisoner, who was said to have bilious fever, he asked the druggist, a "reb," in the most *naïve* manner, what was the usual treatment for that disease! Fortunately, during his stay at Elmira, which was not long, there were no drugs in the dispensary, or I shudder to picture the consequences. This department was constantly undergoing changes, and I suspect that the whole system was intended as part of the education of the young doctors assigned to us, for as soon as they learned to distinguish between quinine and magnesia they were removed to another field of labor.

The whole camp was divided into wards, to which physicians were assigned, among whom were three "rebel" prisoners, Dr. Lynch of Baltimore, Dr.

Martin, of South Carolina, and Dr. Graham, formerly of Stonewall Jackson's staff, and a fellow-townsman of the lamented hero. These ward physicians treated the simplest cases in their patients' barrack, and transferred the more dangerous ones to the hospitals, of which there were ten or twelve, capable of accommodating about eighty patients each. Here every arrangement was made that *carpenters* could make to insure the patients against unnecessary mortality, and, indeed, a *system* was professed which would have delighted the heart of a Sister of Charity; but, alas! the practice was quite another thing. The most scandalous neglect prevailed even in so simple a matter as providing food for the sick, and I do not doubt that many of those who died perished from actual starvation.

One of the Petersburg prisoners having become so sick as to be sent to the hospital, he complained to his friends who visited him that he could get nothing to eat, and was dying in consequence, when they made application for leave to buy him some potatoes and roast them for him. Dr. S. not being consulted, the request was granted, and when, a few hours afterwards, the roasted potatoes were brought in, the poor invalids on the neighboring cots crawled from their beds and begged the peelings to satisfy the hunger that was gnawing them.

When complaint was made of this brutality to the sick, there was always a convenient official excuse. Sometimes the fault would be, that a lazy doctor would not make out his provision return in time, in which case his whole ward must go without food, or with an inadequate supply till the next day. Another time there would be a difficulty between the chief surgeon and the commissary, whose general relations were of the stripe characterized by S. P. Andrews as "cat-and-dogamy," which would result in the latter refusing to furnish the former with bread for the sick! In almost all cases the "*spiritus frumenti*" failed to get to the patients, or in so small a quantity after the various *tolls*, that it would not quicken the circulation of a canary.

But the great fault, next to the scant supply of nourishment, was the inexcusable deficiency of medicine. During several weeks, in which dysentery and inflammation of the bowels were the prevalent diseases in prison, there was not a grain of any preparation of opium in the dispensary, and many a poor fellow died for the want of a common medicine, which no family is ordinarily without—that is, if men ever die for want of drugs.

There would be, and is much excuse for such deficiencies in the South—and this is a matter which the Yankees studiously ignore—inasmuch as the blockade renders it impossible to procure any luxuries even for our own sick, and curtails and renders enormously expensive the supply of drugs, of the simplest kind, providing they are exotics; but in a nation, whose boast it is that they do not feel the war, with the world open to them, and supplies of all sorts wonderfully abundant, it is simply infamous to starve the sick as they did there, and equally discreditable to deny them medicines—indispensable according to Esculapian traditions. The result of the ignorance of the doctors, and the sparseness of these supplies, was soon apparent in the shocking mortality of this camp, notwithstanding the healthfulness claimed for the situation. This exceeded even the reported mortality of Andersonville, great, as that was, and disgraceful as it was to our government, if it resulted from causes which were within its control.

I know the reader, if a Northern man, will deny this, and point to the record of the Wirz trial. I object to the testimony. There never was, in all time, such a mass of lies as that evidence, for the most part, could have been proved to be, if it had been possible to sift the testimony, or examine, before a jury, the witnesses. I take, as the basis of my comparison, the published report made by four returned Andersonville prisoners, who were allowed to come North, on their representation that they could induce their humane Government to assent to an exchange. *Vana spes.* Edwin M. Stanton would have seen the whole of them die before he would give General Lee one able-bodied   soldier.

These prisoners alleged (I quote from memory), that out of a population of about thirty-six thousand at that pen, six thousand, or *one-sixth of the whole*, died between the first of February and the first of August, 1864. Now at Elmira, the quota was not made up till the last of August, so that September was the first month during which any fair estimate of the mortality of the camp could be made. NOW, OUT OF LESS THAN NINE THOUSAND FIVE HUNDRED PRISONERS, ON THE FIRST OF SEPTEMBER, THREE HUNDRED AND EIGHTY-SIX DIED THAT MONTH.

At Andersonville, the mortality averaged a thousand a month, out of thirty-six thousand, or one *thirty-sixth.* At Elmira, it was three hundred and eighty-six, out of nine thousand five hundred, or *one twenty-fifth of the whole.* At Elmira, it was four per cent.; at Andersonville, less than three per cent. If the mortality at Andersonville had been as great as at Elmira, the deaths should have been one thousand four hundred and forty per month, or fifty per cent. more than they were.

I speak by the card respecting these matters, having kept the morning return of deaths for the last month and a half of my life in Elmira, and transferred the figures to my diary, which lies before me. And this, be it remembered, in a country where food was cheap and abundant; where all the appliances of the remedial art were to be had on mere requisition; where there was no military necessity requiring the government to sacrifice almost every consideration to the inaccessibility of the prison, and the securing of the prisoners, and where Nature had furnished every possible requisite for salubrity.

And now that I am speaking of the death-record, I will jot down two rather singular facts in connection therewith.

The first was the unusual mortality among the prisoners from North Carolina. In my diary, I find several entries like the following:

Monday, October 3d.—Deaths yesterday, 16, of whom 11 N. C.
Tuesday, October 4th.—"   "   14   "   7   "

Now, the proportion of North Carolinians was nothing even approximating what might have been expected from this record. I commit the fact to Mr. Gradgrind. Can it be explained by the great attachment the people of that State have for their homes?

The second was the absolute absence of any death from intermittent fever, or any analogous disease.

Now, I knew well that many of the sick died from this, and kindred diseases produced by the miasma of the stagnant lake in our camp; but the reports, which I consolidated every morning, contained no reference to them. I inquired at the dispensary, where the reports were first handed in, the cause of this anomaly; and learned that Dr. Sanger *would sign no report, which ascribed to any of these diseases the death of the patient!* I concluded that he must have committed himself to the harmlessness of the lagoon in question, and determined to preserve his consistency at the expense of our lives,—very much after the fashion of that illustrious ornament of the profession, Dr. Sangrado, who continued his warm water and phlebotomy, merely because he had written a book in praise of that practice, although "in six weeks he made more widows and orphans than the siege of Troy."

I could hardly help visiting on Dr. Sanger the reproaches his predecessor received at the hands of the persecuted people of Valladolid, who "were sometimes very brutal in their grief," and called the doctor and Gil Blas no more euphonious name than "ignorant assassins."

Any post in the medical department in a Yankee prison-camp is quite valuable on account of the opportunities of plunder it affords, and many of the virtuous "meds" made extensive use of their advantages. Vast quantities of quinine were prescribed that were never taken, the price (eight dollars an ounce) tempting the cupidity of the physicians beyond all resistance; but the grand speculation was in whisky, which was supplied to the dispensary in large quantities, and could be obtained for a consideration in any reasonable amount from a "steward" who pervaded that establishment.

I ought not to dismiss this portion of my description of matters medical without adding that the better class of officers in the pen were loud and indignant in their reproaches of Sanger's systematic inhumanity to the sick, and that they affirmed that he avowed his determination to stint these poor helpless creatures in retaliation for alleged neglect on the part of our authorities! And when at last, on the 21st of September, I carried my report up to the major's tent, with the ghastly record of TWENTY-NINE DEATHS YESTERDAY, the storm gathered which in a few weeks drove him from the pen, but which never would have had that effect, if he had not by his rudeness attained the ill-will of nearly every officer about the pen whose good-will was worth having.

I ascend from pills to provender.

The commissary department was under the charge of a cute, active ex-bank officer, Captain G. C. Whiton. The ration of bread was usually a full pound *per diem,* forty-five barrels of flour being converted daily into loaves in the bake-shop on the premises. The meat-ration, on the other hand, was invariably scanty; and I learned, on inquiry, that the fresh beef sent to the prison usually fell short from one thousand to twelve hundred pounds in each consignment. Of course,

7

when this happened, many had to lose a large portion
of their allowance; and sometimes it happened that the
same man got bones only for several successive days.
The expedients resorted to by the men to supply this
want of animal food were disgusting. Many found an
acceptable substitute in rats, with which the place
abounded; and these Chinese delicacies commanded
an average price of about four cents apiece—in greenbacks. I have seen scores of them in various states of
preparation, and have been assured by those who indulged in them that worse things have been eaten—
an estimate of their value that I took on trust.

Others found in the barrels of refuse fat, which were
accumulated at the cook-house, and in the pickings of
the bones, which were cut out of the meat and thrown
out in a dirty heap back of the kitchen, to be removed once a week, the means of satisfying the crav-
ing for meat, which rations would not satisfy. I have
seen a mob of hungry "rebs" besiege the bone-cart,
and beg from the driver fragments on which an August sun had been burning for several days, until the
impenetrable nose of a Congo could hardly have en-
dured them.

Twice a day the camp poured its thousands into the
mess-rooms, where each man's ration was assigned
him; and twice a day the aforesaid rations were characterized by disappointed "rebs" in language not to
be found in a prayer-book. Those whose appetite was
stronger than their apprehensions frequently contrived
to supply their wants by "flanking"—a performance
which consisted in joining two or more companies as
they successively went to the mess-rooms, or in quietly

sweeping up a ration as the company filed down the table. As every ration so flanked was, however, obtained at the expense of some helpless fellow-prisoner, who must lose that meal, the practice was almost universally frowned upon; and the criminal, when discovered, as was frequently the case, was subjected to instant punishment.

This was either confinement in the guard-house, solitary confinement on bread and water, the "sweat-box," or the barrel-shirt. The war has made all these terms familiar, except the third, perhaps; by it I mean a wooden box, about seven feet high, twenty inches wide, and twelve deep, which was placed on end in front of the major's tent. Few could stand in this without elevating the shoulders considerably; and when the door was fastened all motion was out of the question. The prisoner had to stand with his limbs rigid and immovable until the jailer opened the door, and it was far the most dreaded of the *peines fortes et dures* of the pen. In midsummer, I can fancy that a couple of hours in such a coffin would inspire Tartuffe himself with virtuous thoughts, especially if his avoirdupois was at all respectable.

CHAPTER XV.

De minimis.—Withstanding temptation.—The author seeking office.—And getting it.

W HEN the illustrious Anne of Austria entered the city of Paris with her son Louis the Fourteenth, a few words were spoken to her by the President de Bailleul, which, according to the account of "solitary horseman" James, changed the whole after-history of France. So the Constitution of the United States, a venerable instrument, sprang from no more dignified source than a canal project of that genuine Virginian, George Washington. So the fact that Charles I., of England, stammered, cost his majesty his head. So certain architectural speculations of that bull-headed Hanoverian, George III., cost Britain the brightest jewel in her crown. So the absurd weakness of Louis le Jeune, for shaving his chin, precipitated France into four centuries of warfare. So an *old* female Suabian, in the year 1799, threw a pail of water on an excise officer in Northampton County, Pa., and there followed an insurrection which required for its suppression "an army as large as that which captured Burgoyne." In short, that venerable romance, known by courtesy under the name of History, is crowded with illustrations about as veritable as any thing else therein, of the fact that the most important of all matters may spring from causes the most absurdly insignificant.

I have not made these references, oh much-enduring reader of mine, to convict you of incorrigible ignorance in not having known them before, though that would be a laudable motive enough no doubt; nor to make a learned exordium to this chapter, though that would be entirely justifiable, since such things have an air of extreme respectability, and sugar-coat dulness, very much as a flaming caption in a New York newspaper carries off a whole litany of unimportant lies below. In good sooth, my only purpose was to claim credence for an averment I am about to make, by showing that my experience was not exceptional, and that there is nothing absolutely without a parallel, in the declaration, that I owe whatever of peculiar advantage I enjoyed, throughout my whole stay at Elmira, to a sudden attack of that undignified disorder which is treated with copious libations of extract of anise-seed, in infantile victims, and Jamaica ginger and paregoric when the patient gets well out of long-clothes, but which the mature wisdom of adult age finds most certain relief from in Otard or Hennessey *"straight."*

As Napoleon is said to have been a constant victim to this complaint, I need not blush to own that I was similarly afflicted on my arrival at Elmira, and soon wended my way to the drug-store to seek a remedy. Such are the wiles of temperance people, that it will not do to ask, under such circumstances, for a dram, the subterfuges of the Maine Law men having destroyed human confidence to an alarming degree, so I

suggested "ginger" to a mild-looking descendant—
longe intervallo—of Esculapius, whom I found the
presiding genius of the dispensary. I must have
made my request in a super-professional tone, for he
straightway inquired whether I were a practitioner of
medicine. Being among enemies, I exhibited none of
the indignation proper to such an imputation, and
commanding my feelings, merely returned a decided
"No;" but the doctor evidently doubted me still, and
seemed to infer that I must needs have a diploma,
because I knew the *quant. suf.* of Brown's essence;
so he insisted that I should consent to come and aid
him in the daily augmenting duties of his new post.
As, however, I did not have quite impudence enough
to undertake the bolus business, I stoutly resisted, to
the mingled amazement and grief of the surgeon.

He was kind enough to say that he was very sorry
for it, as he would have been glad to have had me
with him. I instantly conceived a high respect for
the doctor's discernment, and told him that I would
be glad to obtain some clerical duties to keep me from
insanity.

The doctor intimated that I might obtain employment at headquarters by making application; whereupon, I framed, in immaculate calligraphy, a note to
Major Colt, requesting him to assign me to some duty,
which, without compromising my position as a hopeless "rebel," would give me employment—something
to eke out the monotonous days of durance. This,
the doctor, in whose eyes I had evidently found favor
—I do not suppose he *meant* an insult by suspecting
me of medicine—undertook to deliver.

Night soon came, and on a French bedstead, composed of a couple of planks, with no bed-clothing of
any description, I stretched myself for a nap. By
about three o'clock, I found it necessary to turn out
to the wood-pile, and seek, in diligent chopping, the
means of restoring the circulation, and, thereupon, I
find the following entry:

"*Elmira, July* 1 3 *th.* —Chopping wood, disgusting.
If I had been that "Woodman," it would have required deuced little singing to have induced me to
"spare that tree," or any other tree."

Day broke at last—and by at last, I essay to express
the fact, that it seemed about as hard to break as
Colonel N.'s passion for wearing clothes that won't fit
him—and shortly after roll-call I received a summons
to the major's tent. He offered me a cigar, which,
having no small vices, I declined, and soon entered
into a free conversation on matters military, political,
and personal, concluding by handing me a note, which
I found to be an assignment to duty in the office of
his adjutant. I reported at once, and was soon at
work transferring to a large "Dooms-day Book" the
record of the name, regiment, company, place and
time of capture, ward and number of each prisoner,
a volume which finally swelled to colossal proportions.
I subsequently found that my position entitled me to
a couple of cups of coffee, and a fee of—ten cents *per
diem!* The coffee was an anomalous production,
made by suspending a bag of ground coffee (?) in a
boiler, holding, I presume, a hundred gallons, the
water in which was renewed for three days, when the
bag was taken out, emptied, and refilled. The first

day's boiling was fair, the second unfair, the third a mockery and a delusion; but such as it was, I accepted it very thankfully, and considered myself entitled to make no complaint, as the Yankee sergeants, in the pen, were furnished with the same.

In the course of a few days, the finances of the prisoners required attention, as money began to be sent them, and the ledger was intrusted to my keeping, and ere long this business became so onerous that a reorganization of the department took place; three professional book-keepers were employed, and a miscellaneous *rôle* of duty was assigned me—making out the morning death-report, answering letters sent to the major, making various inquiries respecting the camp, keeping the sutler's daily accounts straight, and thrice a month making out the "detail accounts" of the prison. As to this latter matter, Elmira formed an exception, I believe, to other Yankee prisons. All duty performed by prisoners, except the police of the quarters—that is, the daily cleaning of the camp—was paid for at the rate of five cents a day for mere laborers, and ten cents for clerks and artificers. These workmen were divided into four heads, according as they report to the adjutant, the commissary, the surgeon, or the officer commanding the labor detail; and as many as four hundred men in all were thus provided with employment, which relieved them of the horrible *ennui* of imprisonment, and furnished them with the means of securing a moderate supply of tobacco—the universal consolation of *Lee's Miserables.*

I may add that the wages thus earned were, in all

cases, as far as I had the opportunity of knowing, honestly paid. I have a thousand times entered the credits on the ledger to various prisoners, and have seen them draw out their deposits in the form of orders.

In the course of the various changes in my line of duty, I gradually acquired possession of a comfortable room, in which I soon rigged up a bunk, and, greatest blessing of all, formed, through the partiality of Captain Whiton, an alimentary association with the sergeant of the cook-house, the chief baker (resembling the good patriarch Joseph in my prison associations, if in nothing else), and a pair of "rebs" engaged in those establishments, which secured me then, and thenceforth, against any apprehensions on the subject of rations, or any interest in the rise of rats.

My association with the officers commanding the prison gave me, of course, many opportunities of assisting my fellow Confederates, and I had the happiness of being the means of making the stay of many of them less irksome, and their restraints less grievous to bear, without any compromise of their or my principles or position, which were known to be those of a rebel, *sans reproche.*

7*

CHAPTER XVI.

Arcadian experience.—A terrible accident.—Neglect of the victims.
—A note from Madam Ik Marvel.—An observatory.—Loyalty and
sight-seeing.—Preaching in camp.—The campaign in a diagram.
—A reminiscence of Jeb Stuart.—The negroes on guard.—Petersburg in flames.—Heavy eating.—Chess.

I RESUME my extracts from my diary, occasionally
anticipating events of subsequent dates referring to
subjects treated of also under a preceding one, to
avoid repetition.

Tuesday, July 12*th.*—Having staked out my sleeping premises, I indulged in the luxury of a good
scrubbing, for myself and my inside clothing and the
sun being warm, I spread both—the clothes and their
wearer—on the grass to dry. At four P. M. dinner was
announced—deuced fashionable up here—tin-plates,
knives and forks, plenty of soup and bread, and beneficent gentlemen in blue clothes politely inviting us to
"ask for more," if we had not enough. We all *asked.*
Not that we were hungry, but merely to satisfy ourselves that the thing was real.

All this over, our captain benignly informs us that
at five o'clock he will take us to the Chemung to
bathe! Some unregenerate rebel, prepared to expect
any thing after his experiences so far, asks him du
biously, "if they furnish Windsor soap and towels,"

and affects much indignation at the laugh he provokes, and a little disappointment at the negative response.

One by one, and that speedily, all these little luxuries vanished. Gone were our tin-plates; gone the knives and forks; gone the seats at, the tables; gone the encouragement to cry out for more; gone the ablutions in the placid Chemung.

"We hardly knew them, ere we sighed farewell."

Saturday, July 16*th.*—An ugly rumor prevails in camp, that a fearful accident occurred yesterday on the Erie Railroad—the train bringing prisoners here colliding with a coal-train going east, near a place called, I think, Shohola. The deaths, it is said, number sixty-seven, and among them are seventeen of the Yankee guards. To-night, we were roused about midnight, with a request that we would come and help the wounded in, the train having arrived with the surviving victims of the catastrophe. Many of them were in a horrible condition, and when I went to the hospital the following Monday I found the wounds of many still undressed, even the blood not washed from their limbs, to which, in many instances, the clothing adhered, glued by the clotted gore; still, the Advertiser, the administration paper in Elmira, of this morning, proclaims to the world that, the poor fellows were humanely cared for! Lieutenant H., who visited them on Tuesday, and who expressed to me his indignation, in no measured terms, at the neglect, could tell a different story. An attempt was made to court-martial this officer for acts of kindness to the prisoners, but he put a stop to all proceedings at once, by intimating to the authorities, that in the event of a trial, he had a story to tell the Herald of the inhumanity of the hospital treatment at Elmira, which a trial would certainly force into print. *He was not molested.*

For many weeks afterwards, friends and relatives tried to obtain admission into the prison to see and administer aid to the sufferers, but were denied the privilege. In one case a very near female relative made a trip of hundreds of miles to see a prisoner, and the only indulgence she received was a permission to ascend an observatory near the "pen," on a certain hour in the afternoon, when her kinsman was allowed to post himself under a tree in the inclosure, with a white handkerchief around his arm, and thus, at a distance too great for any communication, they were allowed *to gaze at each other* for an hour! While I was at Elmira, I remember but two or three instances in which any one was allowed to visit a prisoner. A lady, by dint of great exertions, obtained from the authorities at Washington permission to visit her son, who was badly wounded; and a clergyman, by officiating in the "pen" (a little arrangement of which Major Colt deserves the credit), got the opportunity of a brief conversation with his son. One or two similar cases finished the chapter.

I must not forget to record here the humanity with which the maimed and mangled prisoners were treated by the "Copperheads," near the scene of the disaster, many of whom, as the prisoners informed me, urged upon those who were unhurt, or not too badly wounded to travel, to seize the chance then offered them to escape. Without money, and with hundreds of miles of an enemy's country between them and freedom, there was little encouragement to accept this well-meant counsel. Not more than four escaped.

Friday, July 2 2 d.—Major Colt placed in my hands to-day, for reply, a letter from Mrs. D. G. M., making inquiries concerning certain members of the Fourth South Carolina Cavalry. I had the good fortune to be able to answer her question; and I notice the fact, since it gives me the occasion to speak of the exceeding kindness of hundreds of northern ladies to prisoners. There was a society in Baltimore, composed of the noblest women of that noble city, some of whom denied themselves every luxury becoming their education and position in life, that they might contribute what was thus gained to soothe the sorrows of the gallant boys who had lost their liberty in a cause, which, however proscribed and over-matched, was inexpressibly dear to these good women.

That God who blessed the proffered cup of water cannot pass unheeded such noble and devoted benefactors.

Our curiosity has been excited for some days past, by noticing a wooden structure, consisting of two large platforms, one above the other, which has been going up across the road that bounds one face of our prison. I learn, to-day, that it is an "Observatory," where the sight-seeing penchant of the "Yanks" is to be made available, to put money in the purse of an enterprising partnership, which proposes to turn our pen into a menagerie, and exhibit the inmates to the refined and valorous people of the Chemung Valley, at the moderate fee of fifteen cents a head! *"Re-freshments provided below."*

The event justified the wisdom of the venture, for one of the proprietors, who was part of the management in our pen, assured me that the concern paid for itself in two weeks. I am surprised that Barnum has not taken the prisoners off the hands of Abe, divided them into companies, and carried them in caravans through the country, after the manner of Sesostris, and other antique heroes, turning an honest penny by the show.

So profitable was this peculiarly Yankee "institooshun," that a week or two thereafter a rival establishment, taller by a score of feet, sprang up, and a grand "sight-seeing-and-sprucebeer" warfare began, which shook Elmira to its uttermost depths. One building was Radical, the other Copperhead; one was taller, the other older and more original—qualifications considered important by Dr. Sands, and quite as apropos to sight-seeing as to sarsaparilla. Heaven knows where it all would have ended, but that the Government confiscated the "Democratic platform," under the plea of military necessity, and its Abolition brother remained master of the situation.

Here, every summer afternoon, the population of Elmira—chiefly of the female persuasion—congregated to feast their eyes on their enemies, much after the fashion that the worshippers of Dagon mocked the mighty son of Manoah; and until the days became so cold that exposure in so high a position was unpleasant, the shin-plasters rolled in, and the lemon-pop and ginger cakes rolled out of the orthodox observatory, to the great pecuniary comfort of the true-believers who owned it.

Patriotism is spelled with a "y" at the end of the first syllable up here.

Sunday, July 24th.—Major colt suggested, yesterday, that it might be desired by some of the prisoners to have divine service regularly on Sunday; and added, that if an application were made out, he would forward it to Colonel Eastman, who commanded the post, and who would doubtless approve it. This was done, and the clergymen of the city readily assented to the proposition to visit the prison alternately. Under this arrangement we had service this evening, and almost every Sunday afternoon thereafter. The abolition editor in Elmira complained very bitterly of the alacrity with which the clerical gentlemen accepted the proposal, and intimated that it was due to their *curiosity,* not their zeal,—a little quarrel I do not pretend to adjust.

The first minister who visited us was Rev. Thomas Beecher, a brother (he had a dozen or so, all preachers) of the notorious Henry Ward, who cultivates politics, preaching, and potatoes, to much temporal advantage, as the world knows. "Tom" is not as "sound on the crow" as Ward, and gave us a very practical, sensible, and liberal talk. During his sermon, six hundred and twenty-five more prisoners arrived, and, indeed, they began to come in pretty rapidly now—three hundred on the 25th, seven hundred and thirty-five on the 29th, and so on.

I saw a man to-day, a "reb," ask a negro to give him the quid of tobacco he was chewing when he was done with it, that he might dry it and then smoke it, and the incident furnished me with as much food for reflection as did the little prison flower to the poor prisoner of Saintine's beautiful story. We hear a great deal of the ignorant Irish, the stolid Dutch, etc., but it is my deliberate conviction that the French Academy, if put on thin soup and prison regimen, and deprived of books, papers, etc., for three months, would relapse into Hottentotish heathenism.

A flag-staff was raised to-day, and our drum-corps, a "rebel band," brought out to salute the "astral" with hail Columbia. It is a beautiful banner, un-questionably. Got a peep to-day at the July number of the Atlantic Monthly, which contains an account of Grant's doings so far, illustrated by a diagram curiously illustrating the fact that he has been beaten every time he has met Lee. It consists of the routes of the respective armies sfrom Orange Courthouse to the James. Grant's route is described by a series of arcs, of which Lee's route forms the chords. Starting from Orange Courthouse, they met in the Wilderness, when Grant is driven off into space, and curves back to Spottsylvania Courthouse, when, again repulsed, he flies off on a larger curve to meet Lee at North Anna, and again makes a comet leap, crossing the James. Yet, alas, the struggle cannot last forever. The last regiments have come to the gallant old Knight of Arlington, and he who gloried in the past two years to meet McClellan, Burnside, and Hooker on the plain, fights now "always behind breastworks." He must husband his little handful, that they may last as long as possible against the fresh legions which the draft and the emigrant ships are pouring into the camp of his adversary.

Monday, August 1st.—Got an illustrated paper with a likeness and sketch of the life of General J. E. B. Stuart, this morning. A year ago to-day, I was playing chess under a tree, a mile or so to the left of Culpepper Courthouse, when a courier dashed up to General Mahone's tent, a few yards off, and in a moment orderlies were hastening to regimental headquarters, and the "long-roll" soon brought the brigade under arms. We had heard cannonading frequently during the day, and learned that the Yankee cavalry had crossed the Rappahannock, and were engaging our troopers who had been left to cover the rear of General Lee's army, then on its way to Orange. Anderson's division brought up the rear of the infantry, and Mahone's brigade the rear of the division, so that we expected to move in the morning. It turned out, however, that the Yankees were too numerous for our cavalry to handle; and we were ordered to go to their relief. My own regiment happened to head this movement, and we were double-quicked at a pace not altogether comfortable, at 97° Fahrenheit, in the direction of the cannonading, which was now growing quite distinct and rapid. We soon came in sight of the belt of woods which skirts, on the west and south, that splendid plain on which the great cavalry review was held the year before, and the Yankees in force appearing, my regiment, with one from Posey's brigade, was ordered to deploy as skirmishers, and advance through the woods. Then, for the last time, I saw Stuart. Gayly cantering along in command of

the skirmishers, with his "fighting jacket" on, and
his hat looped up with a long black plume floating
behind, conspicuous from his fine person and horse-
manship at all times—then doubly so, since the only
man on the field who was mounted—his coolness and
splendid gallantry attracted the attention of all. He
was everywhere along the line, foremost of the foremost, cheering all by his encouraging words and his
fearless conduct—humming an air, or giving an order
with equal nonchalance, he looked

> "From clanking spur to nodding plume,
> A very star of chivalry."

There may be different opinions as to his capacity
to manage large movements of cavalry—strange to
say, there are not ten cavalry heroes in history—but
of his individual courage, his presence of mind in
danger, his burning devotion to the cause, his energy
and his enterprising dash there can be no question.
Praise from an officer of high rank, in a different
branch of service, is always a sweet morsel to the
soldier; and as we drove the Yankees to the river-
bank that evening, I saw many a jaded infantry-man
step out with a lighter pace and a firmer tread, as, with
hat in hand, the gallant trooper saluted our regiment
with, "Handsomely   done,   gentlemen;   *are you not
from Petersburg?"*

He passed on whistling the "Bonnie Blue Flag,"
and no one would have thought that the bold trooper
had been in his saddle from early dawn, and under
fire, for eight hot hours.

Tuesday, August 2 d.—Negroes   on   guard   for   the

first time yesterday, and the usual results followed. The hectoring and bullying of the day culminated in the shooting last night of a feeble old man named Potts, who, I am sure, never gave cause of offence. He was an inmate of No. 21, my ward, and although I saw little of him, I knew him, as all did, as one of the most innocuous creatures in the "pen." He was hailed by one of the interior guards while approaching his ward, stopped, and while standing still was shot down.

Lieutenant Richmond told us a fearful story to-day about the blowing up of three lines of intrenchments, the total destruction of a South Carolina regiment, and furthermore, that Petersburg was in flames!

Strangely enough, no papers are allowed here, a regulation that does not prevail in Point Lookout, and we have to take and be thankful for any thing we can get. Of course I don't believe Richmond.

[It was not long before, by the judicious application of a little "fractional currency," conveyed to me by a feminine genius in the centre of a harmless-looking pin-cushion, that I got the truth of this explosion story. It was THE MINE—that fearful crater—a little northeast of old Blandford Cemetery near Petersburg, where "somebody blundered" on the morning of July 30th, and the American citizens of African scent were butchered like rats in a terrier beleaguered sewer;—one of those days when Mahone's immortal brigade did the duty of an army.]

We are to have cannon planted on the hills around us, as there are two battalions of artillery here; so that if Early keeps on through Pennsylvania to the New

York line, as some of the Yankees appear to fear, any mutinous symptoms in the "so called," may at once be checked.

Old Jubal is playing the mischief with the Conestoga horses, and the Rochester Democrat asks, with an affectation of innocence which is very edifying, "What Federal general has burned a defenceless town?" This is very severe on Early for burning Chambersburg. But the Democrat obviously knew very little of the war. A hundred towns, from Hamilton, North Carolina, all across the country to the western verge of Missouri, had been burned by Federal generals before old Jubal thought of levying tribute on Chambersburg. And the men who fired that town had marched in Virginia through many a burned village from Jarratt's Depot to Fairfax Courthouse.

Our black guards (the printer will be careful not to join the words), went off to-day. This incident and the performances of a gaunt Mississippian, divided the interest of the camp. The sutler has gingerbread for sale, which comes in sheets about twenty by twenty-four inches in surface and over an inch thick. Our Mississippi friend asked the sutler why he broke them up.

"To have them of a convenient size for use."

" I think they are a very nice size now."

"Well, I'd like to see you eat one."

"Hand your horse-cake over, old fellow."

And in presence of a crowd of exulting "rebs," who consider the sutler's loss their gain, Mississippi bolted four hundred and eighty cubic inches of gingerbread.

Talk about one ration a day for that stomach!

There are six regiments (*on dit*) of New York militiamen on duty here as our guard.

News of some victory was received here, and in its honor a salute of eleven guns was fired to-day.

Took refuge from the uncomfortable reflections incident to the hearing of a Yankee salute, by beating a Federal surgeon any number of games of chess.

CHAPTER XVII.

Sermons.—A political bloodhound of Zion.—Clothing proscribed.—
Disgusting obscenity.—The Tallahassee.—A comrade dies.—A
contraband.—More restrictive orders.—A sharp retort.—Scurvy.—
A note by "underground."—Awful mortality.—Digging out.—
Pursuit fruitless.

Sunday, 14th.—Had two sermons to-day. One in
front of the observatory, by Reverend Father Kav-
anagh, a Catholic priest—a Christian discourse; the
other by a Reverend Bainbridge, a freedom shrieker,
in front of the major's tent. Bainbridge's speech was
one long insult to the prisoners. Indeed,his conduct
was so disgusting that Lieutenant Richmond, hereto-
fore in this chronicle *honorably* mentioned, presented
the worthy with *ten dollars,* in testimony of his appreciation! The joke was that Bainbridge was fool
enough to publish Richmond's letter in the Elmira B.
R. organ—a gratuitous advertisement of a fool and a
knave. *Arcades ambo.*

During the delivery of B.'s harangue, some of his
auditory quietly rose and left the presence of his
abolitionship; whereupon Richmond arrested the non-
conformists, and but for the intervention of another
officer, would have clapped them in the guard-house,
for the unpardonable sin of unwillingness to receive
gratuitous insult. The clerical world in Puritan-dom

has not changed altogether from the happy days of Quaker whipping and Papist hanging, whereof the annals of Connecticut orthodoxy are rife.

I should be glad to be able to present the reader with the correspondence between Bainbridge and Richmond, but I have lost it.

R. being a negrophilist to the extent of his very limited capacity, greatly belauded the Africanism of B.'s harangue, while B. replied with an unction that nothing but a ten-dollar note could inspire in such a soul.

While on the subject of the disposition of parties unconnected with us officially, I take occasion to make grateful acknowledgments to the mayor of Elmira, John Arnot, Esq., and his most estimable sister. They were noble representatives of a class neither few in numbers nor unimportant in influence throughout the North, with whom charity to an unfortunate people fighting for the right of self-government against far greater odds than their forefathers encountered in the same battle ninety years before, was not considered inconsistent with the obligations of good citizenship.

Thursday, August 18th.—An order was received here to-day from Colonel Hoffman, the commissary-general of prisoners (but emanating from the vindictive breast of Stanton no doubt); prohibiting the sutlers from selling any more food or clothing to prisoners; prohibiting all eatables from being sent into the camp by any party whatsoever; and also forbidding any clothing from being furnished by any person, "except one change of under-clothing, and one suit of a *coarse gray material*" to each prisoner.

A dozen or two of the prisoners were getting blankets and overcoats in anticipation of the coming winter, whose rigors will so far exceed any thing to which most of them are accustomed, that dire suffering must result. Stanton could not endure that.

I obtained to-day several of what they call "family papers"—newspapers published weekly for circulation in the *families* of the good loyal people of the North— and was very much struck with a novelty which has been introduced into them since the war began,—advertisements of obscene pictures, and what are called among men "fancy" articles. These papers teem with them, and nothing could more forcibly illustrate the debauchery of the people. Its effect is visible among the officers and men around us, the daily conversation of many of whom would disgrace a brothel. The hearts must be extremely corrupt which could inspire such foul utterances.

In this respect, as well as in the matter of profanity, there was no comparison between the two armies. I heard more oaths, and far more vulgarity of speech, from Federal soldiers during the five months of my captivity, than I heard in Dixie during the two-and-three-quarter years of my connection with Lee's army; and the evidence is overwhelming, that the immorality, of which there were many examples, tainted much of Northern life. More than one of the officers of the post assured me that there were one thousand prostitutes in Elmira, while it continued a depot for drafted men; and from more than one surgeon I heard statements of the proportion of their soldiers who suffered from venereal taint, which surpassed any thing in the recorded military statistics of the world. The developments on this head with which the Northern press has teemed since hostilities have ceased, the appalling lists of divorces for adultery, the crimes of violence traceable to lust, are too well known to need recital here. I found in the May number of Harpers' Magazine an article deploring this horrible corruption among the young, referrible in great part to this source; and since my return I have seen a thousand evidences in Northern papers of the almost universality of this particular form of vice.

Friday, August 1 9*th.*—To-day another batch of prisoners arrived. They were brought through by land, to avoid falling in with the Tallahassee, which is playing the devil with Yankee shipping, almost within sight of New York harbor. The greatest panic prevails in Gotham thereanent.

August 2 0*th.*—A heavy mail from Dixie, which we can't get, because some villanous "reb" made away with the bulletin-board last night! The adjutant vows that, until the plank comes back, the letters must lie in his desk, and great is our grief thereat.

August 2 1*st.*—This morning the missing plank came back, ornamented with a well-executed checkerboard, whereby some enterprising Confed., disgusted with prison monotony, doubtless supposed he would be allowed in peace to regale himself.

One painful episode mars the record of this month. On the 21st of August, one of our comrades, a young man of irreproachable character, of intelligence, and of a gentleness of manner which won all hearts, even among the enemy, sank under an attack of intermit-

8

tent fever, and died. Major Colt, who had been as considerate as possible during his illness, and who had permitted us to procure any thing the town afforded that he needed, ordered a metallic coffin for him, and allowed a hearse to enter the gates for the conveyance of the body to the potter's field, where the prisoners are accorded their stinted share of "God's Acre." Rev. Arthur Edey, a Confederate chaplain, of one of the Texas regiments, and a decided rebel, though a native of New York, read the impressive service of the Episcopal Church over the remains; while a little group of bareheaded men stood together around "the dead-house," in whose front the body lay. This over, we formed in procession behind the hearse, and marched as far as the prison-gate—all the indulgence we could procure—with heavier hearts, I ween, and far more of genuine respect, than has often marked the obsequies of king or kaiser.

How many of us might make our exit from our prison-bars on this wise, and who should be the next thus followed, were questions that did not fail to suggest themselves to all, and questions which kept some faces solemn for days thereafter.

The last three mails have brought three envelopes to me, each one containing only the signature of the writer. The letters were probably a line or two over the orthodox length, and therefore contraband.

I do not know that I shall have a more appropriate occasion than the present to give place to a colored patriot who performed orderly duties in the pen for the major. His name was Bonus, and he belonged, as he informed me, to a Mr. Posey, of Hendersonville,

Kentucky, from whom he was taken by some passing officers, who wanted a servant and did not care to pay for one.

Bonus was an exceedingly good-natured fellow, and had been evidently a well-trained servant, but the army had spoiled him pretty effectually. He did me a good many services, for which I compensated him as well as I could, but his work for me had the unction of a labor of love, and he did not hesitate to express his preference for "Southern gentlemen."

I went down to the cook-house one evening for my dinner, and found Bonus getting himself up with extreme elaborateness. His boots were as glossy as his cheeks—and this exhausts praise—he sported a brilliant paper collar, a crimson scarf, and a uniform almost new.

Of course I desired to know the cause of all this preparation, a surmise crossing my mind that he was about to enlighten the dulness of republican minds in Elmira by a speech, after the manner of his brother Douglass. So I asked—

"What's the matter, Bonus?"

"Gwine to be married, sir!"

"Married! the mischief! You told me you had a wife in Kentucky, and another in Cincinnati, already."

"Oh yes, sir, but I ain't got none in Elmiry!"

Bonus evidently thought this concluded the argument, as he delivered himself of a self satisfied guffaw, while he completed a "miwaculous tie."

I asked him next morning what he thought when the parson made him promise to cleave to his present wife and forsake all others, inasmuch as he declared he loved his first wife best?

"Oh," said Bonus, "I didn't say nuffin, but I had my 'pinion 'bout dat."

August 28*th.*—The regulations of the pen are growing more strict. No food is permitted to be sold to us by the sutler. That which is sent to us from outside is confiscated, ostensibly for the use of the hospitals, but when Major Colt's back is turned the officers do the confiscating on their private account. To-day I was at the major's tent when a box was opened containing pears for one of the prisoners. Of course he was not permitted to have them, and the Yankee officers began eating them before the boy's face—he could not have been more than seventeen. One of the Yanks remarked with a sneer, "I wish they would send better fruit!"

This was rather too much for "rebel" temper, and the boy retorted instantly—

"My sister did not suppose she was putting them up for Federal officers, I reckon!"

The pear-thief almost blushed.

Last night two prisoners were captured in a tunnel under one of the hospitals. They had almost com- pleted their labor, when they were found out and locked up in solitary confinement.

Monday, 29*th.*—Some clothing arrived to-day. Major Colt being absent on leave, Peck, the purloiner of rings and chains, is in command.

Anticipating the early approach of cold weather, I thought I would apply for a jacket. The ring-thief refused. Said I was "not ragged enough yet."

Wednesday, 31*st.*—An order received to-day prohib- iting the officers from reading newspapers to prisoners.

Cannon-firing to-night in Elmira—a salute over the nomination of McClellan by the Chicago Convention. Sentinels ordered to carry to the guard-house every one who speaks to them.

Sunday, September 4th.—Bishop Timon, Catholic bishop of Buffalo, preached to-day in surplice and cape on that sublime and suggestive text, "I thought of the ancient days. The eternal years were in my mind."

Sunday, 11th.—The restricting of the prisoners to a uniform diet of bread and meat, and denying them the privilege of purchasing other food, are showing their effects in an epidemic, almost, of scurvy.

A thorough examination of the camp has been made during the past week, and the surgeons' consolidated report, as the clerk at the dispensary has just informed me, announces *eighteen hundred and seventy* scorbutic cases out of nine thousand three hundred prisoners.

Last evening the boys, to the number of a hundred, were holding a debating society, when Lieutenant McC. passed by. The president, seeing him eyeing the crowd, invited him to come and take a seat. He was hunting an affront at all times, and took this for one. "No," said he, "d—n you, I'll move on, and if I get any impudence from you, I'll disperse ye d—n quick— the whole of ye."

He would listen to no explanations, and the meeting waited in solemn silence until the great man passed.

The authorities have peremptorily refused permission to establish a school here. A number of us who had assurances that books would be furnished us, requested permission to organize elementary schools for those who could not read or write, and seeing no possible objection, made application for leave, without a doubt of success. Major Colt approved the request, but higher authority forbade.

In order to furnish light to the sentinels at night, and prevent efforts at escape, a number of kerosene lamps are hung up around the inclosure, which are extinguished every morning at dawn by a detail of prisoners. This morning, while engaged in this duty, one of them was hailed by the nearest sentinel with a low whistle, and when he stopped, the soldier threw a note to him and passed on. Picking it up, he found it was addressed to me. Contraband, of course. How it got to the sentinel, I have not been able to surmise.

One of the men who died to-day in the room where our comrade B. is lying, told his brother, almost with his last breath, to tell his family he died of *starvation*. I told this to Captain Munger, who made this characteristic reply:

"It takes all a surgeon's time and capacity to do justice to this camp, and if his brain is seven by nine, he wants help."

The daily death-list is increasing rapidly, and although they are building hospitals continually, there is never room enough.

Wednesday, 21st.—The deaths yesterday were *twenty-nine*. Air pure, location healthy, no epidemic. The men are being deliberately murdered by the surgeon, especially by either the ignorance or the malice of the chief.

Dr. Graham assured me that he stopped one of the attendants to-day who was carrying to the dispensary the prescriptions for *sixty-five beds,* and he had but *two.* The other sixty-three the surgeon in attendance only *looked at.*

Of fourteen men in one of Dr. Martin's sections, twelve were dead; and of seventeen in another, fourteen had died, and two more were certain to die, from the want of food and medicines. He illustrated to me the ignorance of one of the doctors, by declaring that, for a clear case of inflammation of the bowels, he prescribed a styptic so powerful that it is used to stop hemorrhage! Both of these gentlemen have refused to send any more patients from their wards to the hospitals, as death is almost certain to supervene. As I went over to the first hospital this morning early, there were eighteen dead bodies lying naked on the bare earth. Eleven more were added to the list by half-past eight o'clock!

And thus the weeks rolled by. With the outside world we had little in common—cities were surrendered, States overrun, conventions held, battles won, the immortal roll of glory received the names of Polk, Chambliss, Morgan, Rodes, Gregg, and to the vast record of the unnamed heroes were added thousands as worthy of memory as the noblest of these. A new throne was set up on this continent—another turn in that great kaleidoscope which never changes the nature of one bead or bit of glass, be the changes in combinations of position ever so radical and numerous. But to us the book of events was sealed. Occasionally, by a bribe, we would achieve the reading of a newspaper, and hear, in such partial phrase as prejudice affords, the story of the great tragedy our comrades were playing; but the last details, the points of personal interest—who was wounded, who promoted, who *dead* among those with whom we had shared march and camp, bivouac and battle-field— above all, what individual havoc the battering of our little city had occasioned—whom those sweet harbingers of union and amity, the shells of Grant, had sought out and destroyed,—these were unanswered questions, big with import to us all.

Yet a fairer summer never blessed the eye, and as we lolled on the grass in the long, dreamy autumn evenings, indulging *les délices du far niente,* nature seemed to whisper in every passing cloud and sighing breeze, a protest against the fatal strife that was desolating the land.

Early in September an addition was made to our comforts in the shape of a contribution on the part of some benevolent persons in New York, of two hundred or three hundred volumes, wherewith a prison library was formed, and the rush for reading was boundless. Of course these volumes were as diligently expurgated as though the official "let it be printed" adorned the title-page; still, in our circumstances, a play-bill or a price current would have been interesting, and the shelves were soon denuded of every thing, down to infantile toy-books and dilapidated geographies.

> "Linquenda tellus, et domus et placens
> Uxor, neque harum quas collis arborum
> Te præter invisos cupressos
> Ulla brevim dominum sequetiur."

Surely these beautiful words were never written in
a prison. Nor as in "L'Alceste,"

> Ce sont les douceurs de la vie
> Qui font les horreurs du trépas.

About this time, two attempts at escape by tun-
nelling were made—the first a failure, the second successful. By the latter, eleven enterprising beavers
made their escape on the night of the 6th of October.
They commenced digging in the middle of their tent,
which was near an angle of the pen, and conveying
the earth in blankets to the lagoon in the night, they
avoided detection until a hole about thirty feet long
and three feet in diameter was completed, under the
fence, and on the first moonless and cloudy night that
offered, they escaped.

Captain Munger, Lieutenant McConnell, and Sergeant-Major Rudd were at once dispatched after the
fugitives, but they returned on the third day without having found a trace of them.

The weather now grew very cold, and the men,
especially the thousands who were lying on the ground
in tents, began to suffer severely, many of them being
almost, if not quite, destitute of necessary clothing.

Many of the men have been vaccinated also with
virus from patients with venereal disease, and are
suffering from the most loathsome sores produced in
consequence. I will not suspect any human being of
the infamy of thus deliberately poisoning innocent and
helpless prisoners by the hundred, but the effect to
the poor rebels is the same, whatever the intent of
the poisoners. Several have entirely lost the use of
their arms from this cause.

8*

CHAPTER XVIII.

Exchange rumors.—A subterfuge.—Unfit for duty for sixty days.—
Apply for a nurse's post.—Rebel no reproach.—Tricks to obtain an
exchange.—Paroling the sick.—Off for Dixie.

October 1*st.*—For several days past, the rumor has
been current in camp that an exchange of the sick
and wounded on both sides is on the carpet, and the
knowing ones are rubbing up their old complaints,
getting their asthmas, rheumatisms, lame legs, etc., in
working order for the examination about to take
place. What wonder that many a paling eye flashes
up now with unusual fire, and many a poor, feeble
pulse, that for weeks past has been fighting an unequal battle with fever, starvation, memory, and despair, bounds now with a fresh impetus, as in the distance, not very remote, there looms up the enchant-
ing vision of wife and child, mother, sister—HOME.
Many, alas! who are indulging themselves with this
fair prospect, will turn their trembling, tottering feet
towards another home ere the light of the earthly
one can answer their longings. *Pulsat pede.*

To-day the rumor takes definite shape as the surgeons make their rounds through the wards examin-
ing the sick, and excluding from the roll all but those
whose convalescence is apparent, and those who will
never get better *here;* and it leaks out that the order

from Washington is that a list must be made of those
only who will be *unfit for duty for sixty days*. Having beat up England, Ireland, Scotland, France, Ger-
many, Switzerland, Asia, and Africa for recruits, these
invincible twenty millions of Yanks admit that they
are still not a match for five millions of Southerners,
and they cling with the tenacity of death to every
able-bodied "reb" they can clutch, lest he may again
enter the Southern army. The negro question, which
they plead as their excuse for declining a general exchange, is all bosh of the first water. The Northern
people, and I speak from long acquaintance with them,
care much less for negroes than we. The instinctive
aversion with which all white races regard the blacks
—an aversion which begins with the traditions of
infancy, when "the big black man" is the bug-a-boo
wherewith rebellious babyhood is terrified into obedience—is in the South modified, if not conquered,
by constant association and the interchange of mutu-
ally serviceable offices. In the North, and wherever
the white and negro live together in the ordinary
condition of society as rivals in labor, competitors for
employment, claimants for equality of privilege, or
contestants for a share of public patronage of any
kind, the interests and instincts of the whites coalesce
to intensify instinctive repulsion into interested hate,
and a degree of intolerance exists, of which we in the
South have no conception. It is the free States which
have made the most odiously discriminating laws
against the free blacks; and it is only in a free State
that such bloody outbreaks against the negroes as
have characterized Chicago and New York could pos-

sibly occur. It is not, therefore, black love but white
fear, which is interposing difficulties in the way of a
general barter of prisoners; and so controlling is this
latter motive that the prisoners at Andersonville might
forever have sung their sorrows to deaf ears, but for
the advent of that crucible of parties and policies—
election day. The McClellan men have proclaimed a
general exchange as a plank in their platform, and
Humanitarianism—sorry I can't use a shorter word,
but the difference between that and humanity is as
great as between Homousion and Homoiousion, which
kept Christendom in hot water for generations—
Humanitarianism, I therefore say, must have its sop.
So the ingenious Yankees make a compromise between justice and expediency by exchanging only
those who will not be fit for fighting until the present
campaign is over! and thus take the wind out of the
Democratic sails, without sending a man to that army
which the veracious Grant affirms is deserting to him
at the rate of a regiment a day!

Individually, my case is pitiable indeed. Full rations of beef, a quiet conscience, and a good digestion,
have left me in an awkward exuberance of health which
precludes all hope of discharge on the ground of unfitness for duty for sixty days. Indeed, I am afraid
that protracted residence here may induce a physical
condition which even the example of Louis le Gros,
Sobieski, and Dixon H. Lewis could not reconcile me
to, and I am forced, therefore, to seek an occasion of
deliverance on grounds not hygienic. It occurs to
me that it is incredible that so many *miserables* will
be sent on a voyage South without attendants as

nurses, and I am resolved to try the effect of an appeal for permission to accompany the sick in that capacity.

October 3 *d.*—The hospital examinations completed, the search for unavailables began to-day in the wards. At ten o'clock, the camp was mustered by companies, and Major Colt, accompanied by the medical staff and clerk to record the names, made a careful inspection on this wise. The prisoners, by company, being in line, Major Colt gave notice that all who desired to be examined must step three paces to the front. Each man thus presenting himself was examined, and those found unfit by reason of age, or sickness, or wounds were recorded, while the rest were sent back sorrowing. This operation, and the making out of the rolls, occupied several days, and nothing else was talked of or thought of in camp. At last, on the 8th, the lists were completed, some fifteen hundred were found "unfit for duty for sixty days"—one-sixth of the whole—and on the morning of the 9th, notice was given that the "paroles" would be taken that day.

I speak in all reverence when I say, that I do not believe such a spectacle was seen before on earth, since the sick, and the maimed, and the afflicted of every sort crowded for help and healing round the Saviour's feet. Four or five officers took the paroles on the long post which ran along the front of the hospitals, and having nothing better to do, I spent an hour or two watching the scene.

As soon as the announcement was made in the various hospitals that the parole lists were ready, those who had been notified that they had been entered for exchange began to crawl from their cots, and turn their faces towards the door. On they came, a ghastly tide, with skeleton bodies and lustreless eyes, and brains bereft of but one thought, and hearts purged of all feelings but one—the thought of freedom, the love of home. On they came on their crutches, on their cots, borne in the arms of their friends, creeping, some of them, on hands and knees, pale, gaunt, emaciated; some with the seal of death stamped on their wasted cheeks and shrivelled limbs, yet fearing less death than the added agony of death in the hands of enemies, when no kindred hand should give them reassuring grasp, as they tottered forth into the dark valley, and their bones should lie in unhonored graves amid aliens and foemen.

Such haggard, miserable, helpless, hopeless wretches I never saw, and I saw more than one consignment of Federal prisoners on *their way* home. Several died between the signing of the paroles and the day fixed for their departure—paroled by an authority that permits no official perfidy to go behind the record.

No news had, up to this time, reached me as to the result of my application for detail as a nurse; and my hopes of deliverance received sundry rude shocks during the week from the announcement, confidently made by one or two of the Yankee officers, that I should be "the last secesh that should leave that pen;" an honorable distinction, for which I was indebted to the circumstance that I was considered the worst "rebel" in camp.

I should say it (now at least), with the strongest self-reproach but *à merveille,* it is impossible for me to get up even a respectable counterfeit of penitence, while I confess that the name of rebel has no terrors whatever for me.

Never, in reading or in life, has the word grated on my ears with the harshness of conclusive reproach. The greatest names in history, science, art, letters, are the names of *rebeels*—rebels to established theories of politics, philosophy, or criticism. Rebellion is the name which Stupidity gives to Progress; it is the name which venerable Error gives to speculating Truth; it is the name which the henchmen of the Dead Past give to the warriors of the Living Present; it is the name which satisfied Ignorance gives to thinking Inquiry; it is the name which Superstition gives to Reform; which Tyranny, in all shapes, gives to Freedom in all it is the name, in fine, whereby *the false* in life, in literature, in government, in morals, in law, in science, essays to prejudge and prejudice *the true*. No creature is too contemptible to brandish this weapon. The King of Lilliput had his rebels. No being is so august as to escape the imputation—the Saviour of the world was called *seditious*.

And if there is nothing in the word to affright a reflecting soul, it brings least terror of all to a Virginian.

What name does my grand old Mother-State hold in honor that is not the name of a rebel? She boasts no heroes that were not rebels. She raises no colossal bronze, save to rebels. When she points to her jewels, they are all rebels. Rebels give names to her public institutions; to her political divisions; to the streets of her cities. Her coat of arms is the pictured triumph of a rebel. The greatest name amid her dead, and the greatest among her living, are the names of rebels. It is the patronym of all her mighty departed, from Bacon to Washington, from Washington to glorious Jackson; it is the title of every famous son she boasts among the living. Vain will be all efforts of Jacobinism to make it odious: it will never bring a blush to a Virginian's cheek who remembers that he shares the title with the dead Ashby and the living Lee.

While, therefore, I feel appropriately glum at the prospect of a winter residence in this Siberian locality, the *cause* of that protracted misery (if rebelliousness, excessive and *prononcè* as our Gallic friends phrase it, be that cause) soothes somewhat the poignancy of my grief, inasmuch as it involves a compliment.

October 9th.—Io triumphe! Evoe! A knock at my door ten minutes after nine; my friend D. calls me out with the gravity of a lord-chancellor, and, *sotto voce,* announces, "Major Colt has just put your name down on the list." Unfortunately, the sumptuary regulations of the pen preclude the orthodox American fashion of expressing unlimited gratification, so I content myself with *feeling* as much joy as is consistent with sanity, and straightway go about disposing of my various unportable chattels among less favored friends —the universal concomitant of emigration.

Little was now done or talked of by any one except the approaching hegira of the lucky candidates for exchange. Many a brawny fellow with the thews of Alcides would gladly exchange his exuberant health and perfect strength, for the most helpless frame and the puniest limbs in the hospital, and numberless expedients to elude the vigilance, or corrupt the integrity of the examiners were practised, and with very encouraging success.

One prisoner assured an examining-surgeon that he was wounded in the arm, so as to make it impossible to carry a musket for more than sixty days. Slily turning up his sleeve, he exposed to the doctor's eyes alone, a five-dollar greenback rolled up. The amiable Galen dexterously removed it, and told the clerk to "enter Mr. B., gunshot wound in left arm."

I was much amused, after my return, with a story told me by the Confederate commissioner of exchange. A stalwart prisoner called to see him on one of those vain hunts after money, which green "rebs" occasionally wasted their time about, when Colonel O. asked him how *he* managed to get off.

"Oh, I had fits, sir."

"Fits! You don't look much like it."

"Oh, yes, sir; I had 'em a half a dozen times a day, towards the last."

"Do you have them, now?"

"Well, no, sir. *There's no occcasion.*"

"Indeed. You *could* have them, then?"

"Yes, certainly. Would you like to see one?"

The colonel expressed his desire for that phenomenon, and in a second his visitor was sprawling on the floor, kicking things about generally, and foaming at the mouth after the most epileptic fashion. In the course of a few minutes his limbs grew rigid, he began to breathe painfully, and he finally stretched himself out

as though utterly exhausted—the only part of the performance that was not feigned.

After lying a moment or two, he jumped up, and
saluted the astonished commissioner with—

"Don't you call that a pretty fair fit, sir, on short
notice? Well, that ain't a first-class one, by no
means."

Thus the poor ones had to rely on their wits, while
the better-off ones bribed.

Bonus, my colored friend, is in great grief to-day
Notwithstanding the moral and Christianizing influences of several months in the Federal army, Bonus,
alas! will steal, and unfortunately does not discrim-
inate enough. Yesterday Lieutenant McConnell lost
one of his revolvers; to-day, Bonus is proved the thief,
and he is tied up for it. To-morrow, he is to go to
the front—the rod held perpetually *in terrorum* over
patriots with little moral idiosyncrasies, like the one
referred to.

By the way, Bonus had some companions in misfortune. Two "rebels" were brought before the
major, on charge of fighting. The fact was proved,
and the punishment was immediately pronounced.
They were tied, back to back, and forced to walk up
and down before the major's tent two hours every
morning, and two every afternoon, until amicable relations were restored. It did not take long. He has
just come in to tell me that he gets off. The reason is
that he is a *Mason!*

This order has spread wonderfully over the country
since the war began, and especially in the North. The
material advantages which it incontestably secures,

have contributed largely to this; but I am persuaded that there is a deeper reason, which I will merely indicate. The course of many of the churches before and during the war, especially in the Northern States, almost destroyed popular reverence for religion, and Masonry, which proposes as high a morality as these churches, offered at the same time indubitably superior worldly advantages. In a word, it was as much of a religion as most of these churches, and much more of a benefit. No wonder it spread. The vilest men make use of it. About the brightest Mason in New England is Ben Butler, which, of course, ends the argument. And while in prison at Elmira, I found that the worst and most worthless men could outstrip the best in a contest for the "good places" about camp, if they were only Masons. All this, however, is only incidental to my purpose, which is to note the omnipotence of the order, and its gigantic influence for good or evil, according as it is well or improperly directed.

Almost all of my Petersburg comrades being old men, easily obtained the entry of their names on the coveted roll, since it was manifest they would be fit for no active duty in the field; and it was the greatest of my delights to anticipate our return in company to the city which had so long mourned our absence, and made so many efforts to procure our special release.

On the morning of the 11th, all being in readiness, the fourteen hundred for exchange were called out alphabetically, and in three squads, at different hours of the day, marched through the city from the pen to the Erie Railroad depot, where two trains of box-cars stood waiting.

I took leave of my companions with the regret with which intimate association, such as that of prison, is sure to tinge the parting of the most callous, and from none with more than the excellent officer and gentleman who commanded the prison. His eyes filled as he bade me good-by at parting, and I fear my own were not altogether dry, as for the last time I wrung the hand of the true man, and humane, courteous official, Major Colt. He handed me a memorandum as we parted, asking my kind offices for Lieutenant-colonel John R. Strang, of his regiment; and I almost felt regret at hearing, subsequently, of Colonel Strang's release, as it prevented me from reciprocating on my return home, in some slight degree, attentions and courtesies, which I, in common with all my Petersburg comrades, had constantly received at the hands of this excellent officer.

CHAPTER XIX.

Leaving Elmira.—The trip to Baltimore.—Seven die on the train.—
Arrival in Baltimore.—Benevolent ladies.—A stratagem.—Off for
Point Lookout.—Official thieving.-Major Brady.—Massachusetts
in 1775.—Stonewall Jackson.—His last fight.—A memory.—
Stonewall Jackson's way.

OUR passage through Elmira did not excite quite
the attention which marked our journey through the
same streets three months before, the curiosity of the
Chemung Athenians having become satiated with such
sights. Many citizens who dared to approach us with
expressions of sympathy accompanied us to the cars,
and ministered as they were able to the comfort of the
most needy, but there was none of the obtrusive following and staring, with which we were honored on
our first appearance.

It was nearly nightfall when we were "all aboard."
A worthy and influential citizen of the town, to whom
I was introduced, loaded me down with sandwiches
and a bottle of Monongahela as I stepped into my
box-car—may the angels make his bed in glory, for
that same—the engine screamed, and off we started
for Dixie. We would scarcely have felt as much ex-
hilaration had we known that the trip would take a
full month.

The events of the next forty hours consist in the

dismal items of a creeping ride over the "Northern
Central" Pennsylvania Railroad, which leaves the
Erie road at Southport, and traverses the most barren and uninteresting region of the Keystone State,
through Harrisburg to the Maryland line, and on to
Baltimore. I remember nothing particularly of this
trip, except that whenever the train stopped, the
guards robbed the nearest orchards; that I slept the
first night in a space of three feet by six inches; that
I consumed fabulous quantities of crackers; that when
I got into Maryland, we found various flags flying in
honor of the vote for emancipation, given the day before; that for slowness of movement, I'll match that
ride against even the traditions of the "old City
Point" road, in my own State—a comparison which
exhausts the resources of reproach.

On my way down I had quite a discussion with a
Lieutenant Rounds, who hailed from a recently discovered locality in the wilds of Maine, and who, like
most people who come out of the desert, had the most
microscopically minute range of vision.

He started out with a very grave and measured
enunciation (he must have been a schoolmaster, I
think) of the proposition that every rebel was murderer, who deserved hanging; and intimated the converse of the proposition, that every Yankee soldier
was a saint, who deserved canonization. Of course
there was little use in formal discussion with such a
homunculus, but I think I broke somewhat the effect
of his speech by forcing him to admit that George
Washington richly deserved hanging likewise—a conclusion to which his reasoning led him so rapidly, that

I made him admit it, greatly to the disgust of his
brother officers, before he had time to invent a pro-
viso which would take that eminent rebel out of the
category of the gibbet predestined.

It is needless to say that the prospect of hanging in
such desirable company reconciled us to the respectability of the thing, however untouched it left the de-
sirableness of that particular route to Styx on other
grounds.

The condition of a long train of box-cars, filled with
such a number of helpless sick, confined in the same
spot, and crowded unnecessarily during a ride of some
two hundred and sixty miles, at the rate of less than
seven miles an hour, can easily be imagined.

Finally, however, we arrived in Baltimore at ten
o'clock on the morning of the 13th, with *seven dead
men* on the train, the first toll of the dread Reaper on
our journey home.

A few ladies and children were at the depot—those
who dared to brave the fines and dungeons, the imprisonment, and insult, and exile, with which humanity
and the natural yearnings of kinship are crushed out
in *loyal* Baltimore; but, I doubt not, there were
thousands of hearts in that fair town that day, who
would have thought it the highest honor to have been
allowed to minister to the sick and dying in our long
trains, and were only restrained from coming by their
unwillingness to witness sufferings that they could not
alleviate, while the mere effort would compromise
them, without aiding us. The train had hardly
stopped, when a gorgeously caparisoned horse and
major dashed into the little crowd of ladies who were

pressing around the car nearest the street, with inquiries about their relatives, and the less noble animal
forced them back with a brutal sneer, and an intimation in decided terms, that a renewal of the experiment of speaking to us would infallibly result in their
being sent to the common guard-house!

I was particularly sorry for this, as I desired to
send a message to a friend in the city, and I resolved
to evade the order prohibiting intercourse. Tearing
a leaf from my note-book, I jotted down a few lines,
and rolling the letter in as small a compass as possible,
I watched my opportunity when the guards were not
looking in my direction, to hold it up with a gesture
that attracted one of the ladies. As soon as a fair
opportunity offered, I shot the "paper pellet towards
her, and was much gratified to observe the diplomatic
nonchalance with which she put her foot on the mis-
sive, quietly continuing her conversation with a female
friend meanwhile. A moment or two afterwards she
accidentally let fall her handkerchief, and stooping to
recover it, picked up my note with it, and conveyed
both to her pocket—all this without a look towards
me. It was several minutes before she honored me
with a glance of intelligence, which satisfied me my
communication was in safer hands than any mail
system in Christendom could furnish.

During the day, for it required all day to get us
from the depot to the dock, several ladies remained
near us; by stratagem, entreaty—any means, and
every means—conveying to the wretched inmates of
our train, coffee, bread, cakes, fruit, tobacco—any
thing in short that money could buy, or woman's

kindness of heart suggest. Among these, a few were conspicuous in their zeal to serve us; and I remember best a courageous woman, with a true Baltimore face, dark eyes, a Southern complexion, lithe, graceful form, and features radiant and mobile with intelligence and beauty, and the divine glory of charity, who spent the long day in these ministrations, unawed by frowns, undismayed by threats, and conquering her native womanly disgust at the vulgar hirelings, that out-stripped even heathen heartlessness in the cruelty and brutality with which they repulsed all efforts at communication with us. Her name in two hemispheres is the synonym of all that is noble, true, and good, and from Pope's day to our own, has formed a proud antithesis to

"——knaves and fools and cowards."

The sun was setting as I jumped on an ambulance well filled with hospital equipage, and rattled off to the wharf, where three steamers were awaiting us—the Thames, the Tappahannock, propellers, and a side-wheeler whose name I have forgotten.

I was a long time getting there, not so much because of the distance as because of the company I was in.

This consisted of the driver (drunk), a Federal guard (drunk), and three rebs, one drunk, the other two merry. All besides myself being familiar with the city of monuments, they amiably concluded to *see a little of the town* before going aboard ship, and if visiting bar-rooms and other attractive places is

9

seeing the town, they saw it, as Artemus Ward would express it, "Slightually, if not more so."

Five bells struck aboard a vessel near us, as our well-loaded steamer, with its ghastly freight of the sick, wounded, and dying slowly moved from the dock. We left behind us, in Baltimore, several of our companions, whose condition was such that their further progress would have been certain death, one of them a gray-haired old man of our own city, who died shortly after, in a Federal hospital in that city —one of the many "unfit for duty in sixty days."

It was nearly dawn when I awoke to find our craft hard aground off Point Lookout; but soon the tide rose, and we steamed up to the dock,—a heavy sea running.

Now commenced the troublesome and dangerous operation of getting the helpless sick ashore. A gangway plank was stretched from the side of the ship to two flour-barrels standing on the dock, and down this "shute" the poor helpless, maimed creatures were slid like coal into a vault. Those of us who were able spent our time in alleviating the roughness of this original process of debarkation, and assisted in placing the sick and wounded in the ambulances which conveyed them to the, hospital, a quarter of a mile distant.

Between the arrival of the first ship and the second, I walked to the hospital, and deposited in the steward's room of No. 8 my "pack," expecting to return and get it when my duties on the wharf were over.

These occupied me, as well as the rest of us, until late in the afternoon, when those of us who did not need immediate hospital treatment (about one-half of the whole number) were ordered to fall into line, and march to the old "officer's pen," the inclosure in which we were temporarily placed prior to starting for Elmira in the preceding July. As the steward of Hospital No. 8 had taken charge of my pack, and promised to keep it for me, I felt little apprehension respecting its contents, but, inasmuch as the nights were already becoming cold, I felt some solicitude about the immediate recovery of my blanket, and asked Captain Munger, one of the officers who had accompanied us from Elmira, to state the case to Major Brady, the commandant, who was standing within a few feet of us, and ask permission for me to go and get my clothing. He was refused so curtly and insolently, that he at once told me, "You need not expect to get your goods, *you see.*"

I bade him good-by, and have not seen him since, nor, perchance, ever will again. Wherever he is, and whatever he does, however, Captain Ben. Munger has the good-will of every prisoner who ever drew rations at Barracks No. 3, on the banks of the Chemung.

I may as well say here, that I made several efforts to obtain my satchel, without avail, for two days, and when I did recover it, every thing valuable was stolen. This petty larceny was committed by a smooth-faced innocent, with a downy upper lip, who at that time acted as orderly for Dr. Thompson, the chief surgeon of the post. Three weeks afterwards, Dr. Thompson returned me one or two of the articles stolen, but allowed (I presume) his underling to keep the rest. This, at least, I know, that I furnished Dr.

Thompson with a full description of the stolen goods, some of which I saw his orderly wearing the day I finally left the Point, but never received any except a trifling proportion of the whole. All this I regretted, mainly, because I lost thereby several beautiful specimens of prison work that I was bringing home to my friends; and the only comfort I received from my comrades, was a sneer at my gullibility in leaving any thing valuable out of my sight when Yankee soldiers were about.

When we were turned into the pen, Brady, whom the tenants of Point Lookout prison were disloyal enough to accuse of superior skill in confiscating their property, and in general *roughness* of demeanor, facetiously conjured us to make ourselves as comfortable as possible.

This was rather a grim joke. The appliances for comfort consisted of a scant supply of tents, to which, after a few days, was added a more scant supply of *straw,* then the water was scant, the rations scant, and every thing else on a scant pattern. When it is remembered that these prisoners were, for the most part, sick men, many of whom had just come out of hospitals, our chance of comfort in open tents, and sleeping on the ground, in the cold humidity of Point Lookout, was about as slim as LL. D. Butler's prospect of paradise, or his various "subjects'" chances for the recovery of their missing silver. Apropos of Ben, I think I have discovered a trace of his revolutionary ancestry in a letter written by Washington to General Lee, which describes, in its final paragraph, that peculiar virtue which has flowered out in such consummate perfection in the Duke of Spoons.

It reads as follows:

"AUGUST 27, 1775.

"I have made a pretty good storm among such kind of officers as the Massachusetts government abounds in since I came to this place, having broke one colonel and two captains for cowardly behavior at Bunker Hill; and two captains for drawing more provisions and pay than they had men in their companies, and one for being absent from his post when the enemy appeared and burned a house just by. Besides these, I have at this time one colonel, one captain, and two subalterns under arrest for trial. In short, I spare none, and yet fear it will not all do, as these people seem to be only attentive to their own interests."

Wednesday, 26th.—Our numbers have been largely increased by arrivals from the other pen of prisoners ordered thence because of unfitness for duty for sixty days, or for the better reason that they had the wherewithal to *bribe out.* We have also been receiving additions from General Early, who, according to Sheridan, has been thrice beaten, with exceeding spoil of war in the Valley of Virginia. Sheridan boasts, with a ferocity which will forever blacken his name in the judgment of impartial history, of the devastation he has inflicted upon the non-combatant population. I have never before read an official report in civilized war in which so great a parade is made of vandalism. The barns and stacks of grain destroyed afford him obviously far more pleasure than his captures either of men or munitions of war. What a crop of hate this conqueror of grist-mills is sowing!

How different this story of robbery and organized plunder from the glories with which the immortal Jackson illumined every hill-side of that long vale of the Shenandoah! When will that marvellous story be written? Is there no one with the genius to comprehend, and the book-craft to do justice to that wondrous episode in this wondrous war—unparalleled save in the dazzling marvels of "The Campaign in Italy." Who will tell, in language worthy of the theme, how, with a few thousand infantry, poorly supplied with every thing but valor and leadership, this illustrious captain swept army after army out of the field, defying numbers, annihilating distance, despising labor, regardless of odds, fairly revelling in the *gaudia certaminis—preferring* to have, it would seem, three armies to fight at the same time, that the glorious boys might not rust with idleness. Brave as "Lion Heart," modest as Sydney, in action as impetuous as Ney, in counsel cautious as Fabius, reticent as Wellington, magnetic as Napoleon—there is not a meadow or mountain-top in all that lovely Valley that is not alive with tribute to this matchless chieftain, and yet, "history" hardly accords his grand campaign a paltry page; and his name, which woke the echoes of two hemispheres, seems doomed to find no more enduring monument than the ephemeral record of hasty pamphleteering, or the fading traditions of the camp fires!

I saw him last in life on the day before his death—the day before he drove the discomfited Dutchmen in wild confusion from the "old church," down to the works of Chancellorsville. Longstreet was hammering fruitlessly away with the larger part of his corps on the Blackwater, when the Federals crossed the Rappahannock with two armies, almost simultaneously, at Fredericksburg and ten miles above. Either army was larger than all Lee had, and how to meet both, on fields so far apart that co-operation was impossible, was the question. Jackson was on the extreme right, but the strongest demonstration was on the extreme left, and there the fight must be made strongest, though Fredericksburg should be lost and the railroad destroyed.

It was the very field for the genius of the great flanker.

In the early gray of the dawn, we, who were watching on the left, saw a double column coming up the turnpike, with the long sweeping stride of practised marchers; and a shout arose, as some one cried out, "Here comes Longstreet's men." But in a few moments a little cavalcade rode up to our picket-line, our beloved Lee at the head, and on his left his great right arm, "Stonewall," and we knew the old hero was to be with us in that fight. The light of victory was already in his eye, and blazing over his habitually calm face. No human countenance ever gave the spectator more thorough assurance of self-reliance— of its ample capacity to confront and conquer any obstacle, no matter how great or how unexpected; and there was a magnetism about the man, the want of which is the only defect in General Lee. It is the very essence of military genius, and no man of such calm demeanor in history ever possessed as much. This is not love or respect, for Lee had full measure of these. It seems to be a subtle power of infusing others with the owner's spirit and will, until they seem to become a part of him. "That's Stonewall, or an old hare," said an old campaigner on the first Maryland march, as he heard peal after peal of yells of delight at the head of the column in which he was moving; and the words expressed the enthusiasm which the familiar face and the shabby suit always inspired.

After a brief consultation with General Lee, Jackson raised his hat and turned away—turned away to glory and to death.

The next morning, at ten o'clock, we were pushing into the abandoned works at Chancellorsville—won mainly by the skill, endurance, and magnificent fighting of Jackson. And Lee came by us, as we hurried through the fortifications to finish our work at Fredericksburg, calm, imperturbable—and Stewart gayly trotting as though on a holiday—and Wright, with his long hair floating behind as he galloped at racing speed along the joyous line, and many another not unknown to fame; but one loved face and form was missing, whose presence in that grimed and bloodstained array would have shaken the solid earth with cheers. Ah! how our eyes moistened as the news then began to spread from van to rear of our hurrying column, *"Jackson was wounded this morning!"*

When I saw him next, old men were weeping like feeble women, and women were wailing with the passionate grief of childhood, as they crowded the capital of Virginia to get, for love and immortal memory, one last long look at *Jackson dead.*

The lays of the South will hardly be written. They are *contraband* now, and will be till the hate of this generation dies, and a new one comes which will be more proud of Jackson than of any of all the names of this war. Be this my apology for putting in this form—more durable perhaps than a newspaper—the best camp-song of the war. To be perfectly candid, our poetic literature was contemptible throughout the struggle. The genius, like the courage and high character of the South, was *in the war,* and with them the struggle for independence through such tribulation was entirely too serious a matter to find rhymes for, and deck out in the luxury of rhythm. But this is a good song, nevertheless:

STONEWALL JACKSON'S WAY.

Come, men, stack arms! Pile on the rails—
　　Stir up the camp-fire bright;
No matter if the canteen fails,
　　We'll make a roaring night.
Here Shenandoah crawls along,
Here burly Blue Ridge echoes strong,
To swell the brigade's rousing song,
　　Of "Stonewall Jackson's way."

We see him now,—the old slouched hat,
　　Cocked o'er his eye askew,—
The shrewd, dry smile—the speech so pat,
　　So calm, so blunt, so true.
The "Blue Light Elder" knows 'em well;
Says he, "That's Banks, he's fond of shell:
Lord save his soul! we'll give him——" well,
　　That's "Stonewall Jackson's way."

Silence! ground arms! kneel all! caps off!
　　Old Blue Light's going to pray;

Strangle the fool that dares to scoff!
   Attention! it's his way!
Appealing from his native sod,
"Hear us, in power, Almighty God!
Lay bare thine arm, stretch forth thy rod,
   Amen." That's Stonewall's way.

He's in the saddle now! Fall in!
   Steady! The whole brigade!
Hill's at the ford, cut off; we'll win
   His way out, ball and blade.
What matter if our shoes are worn?
What matter if our feet are torn?
Quick step! we're with him before dawn!
   That's Stonewall Jackson's way.

The sun's bright lances rout the mists
   Of morning–and, by George!
Here's Longstreet struggling in the lists,
   Hemmed in an ugly gorge.
Pope and his Yankees, whipped before,
"Bayonets and grape!" hear Stonewall roar.
"Charge, Stuart! pay off Ashby's score,
   In Stonewall Jackson's way."

Ah! maiden, wait, and watch, and yearn,
   For news of Stonewall's band!
Ah! widow, read with eyes that burn,
   That ring upon thy hand!
Ah! wife, sew on, pray on, hope on!
Thy life shall not be all forlorn;
The foe had better ne'er been born,
   That gets in Stonewall's way.

CHAPTER XX.

Pen routine.—Diagnosis.—Plundering the prisoners.—Off for Dixie. —The Northern Light.—The Merrimac and Commodore Vanderbilt.—Hampton Roads.—Mitchelltown.—Servus servorum.—A strange history.—Savannah.—Home!

Revenons! The days dragged very wearily here. As we were all nominally sick men, the facetious Yankees put us on sick diet or half rations, and as there was no sutler, and no chance, therefore, of eking out our allowance, we began to fear our enemies were in a fair way of unfitting us for active service for the balance of the war. It seems that we are to be kept here until five thousand are accumulated, and then deported. Having no other occupation, I undertook some duties in connection with the hospital—for we had a hospital within the pen—and thus managed to endure the tedium of my cage by pious exercises in the shape of administering hospital slops and allopathic boluses.

In the midst of the pen was a pile of logs which the prisoners used as an observatory to get the earliest information of the arrival of the "New York," the truce-boat of Colonel Mulford, United States commissioner of exchange, whose coming, it was thought, would insure a speedy exit: but the Yankees took it into their sapient heads that there was something "irregular" in this, and our logs were pulled down and all spying put under the ban.

October 28*th.*—An order came to *diagnose* us to-day, and it became necessary that every one should have a disease forthwith—at least on paper. We were accordingly called up and asked our various complaints: being still in a vulgar condition of health, it became necessary for me to catch a disease suddenly; accordingly, I soon became painfully afflicted, and when called on by the doctor, I drawled out a disease with a name as long as a Nantucket "sea sarpint," and was passed *nem. con.* This looks as though we were about to move, and Dixie stock is rising.

Sunday, October 3 0*th.*—Saturday we had a false alarm. We were ordered out, inspected, examined, and marched down to the dock where, in the offing, the Arctic, Baltic, and Northern Light are lying, and "then marched back again," to our measureless and unspeakable disgust. But to-day we are off in earnest. About eleven A. M. we were summoned into line, our names called, and all our blankets stolen from us, by order of the incomparable Brady, unless they were so worthless as not to be an object. I objected to giving up mine, as I had bought and paid for it, and as it was obvious, on inspection, that it never could have been an army blanket; but the amiable Brady assured me that "if it was not an army blanket it soon should be," and instructed his under-thief to take it.

Having been stripped of these and any contraband articles of clothing, such as an extra coat or pair of pants, we were conducted to the wharf, where a small steamer received us "in lots," and conveyed us to the Northern Light, which, with steam up, was lying about a half a mile out. The other transports were already laden with the most helpless of the prisoners —those who, in the first instance, had been taken to the hospitals.

We scrambled up the side of the fine steamer, formerly a mail and passenger ship in the California trade, then a government transport in the employment of Uncle Abe, at one thousand dollars a day besides her coal, and were marched in various directions to the two lower decks of the ship, where hammocks of canvas had been slung in sufficient number to accommodate nine hundred men. Some twenty or thirty were separated by the surgeon, and kept on deck; for what purpose, we never knew, and our little tug steamed ashore for another load. It was near nightfall when she returned; and, as many of the prisoners were victims of night-blindness, I asked and obtained permission to assist them aboard, the dangerous footing of the ladder inspiring them with uncomfortable apprehension of a plunge overboard—and, although Friar Peyton told Henry VIII. that the road to heaven was as short by water as by land, the same is not as true of the road to Dixie.

I had helped the last one aboard, when a handsome, frank-looking sailor with as genial a face as ever bent over a binnacle, tapped me on the shoulder, and informed me that he wanted to see me "forrerd." My military habit of obedience, I presume it must have been that induced my instant compliance, and under the guide of Samuel H. Rich, first officer of the ship,

I soon found myself in his cabin, scrutinizing the pattern of his furniture through an excellent glass, not a magnifier much—cubical contents one pint; whose make, I never knew. From this time I, in common with all my fellow-prisoners who had any intercourse with him, had occasion to bless the day that we fell into the hand of so clever a gentleman and capital an officer. A young man, but an old seaman, he had circumnavigated the globe a half a dozen times, be the same more or less, knew every foot of sea from Fulton Ferry to Van Diemen's Land, and possessed that ease of manner, that cosmopolitan heart and large fund of information and anecdote which, with thorough professional knowledge, forms the highest type of sailor—almost the highest type of the social man.

The management of the ship devolved on Mr. Rich, during our stay aboard, the captain being sick; and I had thereby occasion to observe the universal respect and good-will which he commanded from the whole crew. These, by the way, were an exceptional party. There was not a Yankee among them, as far as I discovered, and a more liberal set of enemies would be hard to find. As I have spoken of the captain (Lefebre), I may mention that he was the officer who commanded the Vanderbilt when she was down in Hampton Roads, threatening destruction to our Merrimac. When the Merrimac threw all Yankeedom into such confusion early in 1862, Lincoln sent for Commodore Vanderbilt, to advise with him as to what was to be done with the monster. The commodore informed him that there was no use trying to fight her, and the only chance was to run her down; but, as the United

States possessed no vessel of sufficient tonnage for that achievement, he presented Lincoln with the Vanderbilt, a magnificent steamer of six thousand tons, and hurried to New York to put her in order for the great work. She had her upper works at once taken off, a formidable battery of heavy timber and cotton bales put in, enforcing her bows with thirty solid feet of structure, and a heavy casing of cotton bales put around her boilers. In this trim she was sent down to Hampton Roads, and there lay for sixty days; but as the Merrimac challenged the whole Yankee fleet for two days after her arrival, in vain, I presume the naval commandant at Fortress Monroe did not have as much faith as Vanderbilt in the success of the running down project.

Monday, October 31*st.*—Arrived off Old Point this morning. The harbor is filled with vessels of war; among which, I recognize the Minnesota, Susquehanna, Wabash, Shenandoah, Ironsides, and any number of iron-clads, "double-enders," etc., the whole floating, I understand, two thousand guns!

Commodore Lee has been superseded, on account, it is said, of too much love for the rebels, and Porter reigns in his stead. On each side, the war seems to have eliminated natives of the other from its service, until it has become a war of race rather than of institutions. Porter's vessel, the Malvern, lies a mile west of us.

We remained in Hampton Roads until Tuesday, the 8th. The Atlantic and Baltic lay near us, and every morning we saw coffins going over the side in numbers which suggested uncomfortable reflections on the

uncertain tenure of life on a prison-ship. On the Atlantic alone, there were forty deaths during our stay
in the harbor—a stay obviously unnecessary, and
therefore, shamefully cruel, since it compelled the confinement of hundreds of sick men in the filthy and
unventilated holds of large ships without proper food,
medicine, or attendance—the second great toll of the
reaper. Captain Grey, of the Atlantic, protests loudly
against the inhumanity of the procedure, but circum-
locution must have time. On the 2d and 3d, we
were visited by a furious storm, during which Commodore Porter steamed up to Portsmouth, out of the
reach of danger, and there remained until Saturday.
On the 4th, Butler left for New York, whither he goes
to keep the peace! The crew of our ship are from
New York, principally, and all McClellan men—their
indignation at having the brute sent to overawe their
friends of "the bloody Sixth" is quite refreshing, and
they freely promise him a merry time if he interferes.
They are mistaken—no race ever bowed the knee to
bayonets with such edifying humility as our Northern
brethren. If Mr. Davis, under any conceivable pre-
text, had dared to make use of military intimidation
in any one of the scores of cases in which Mr. Lincoln
successfully tried it, he would have been impeached in
twenty-four hours, and yet the world has been, and
will be, filled with terrible stories of the despotism of
the "Slaveholders' Rebellion." Lions no more write
books than they paint pictures.

Saturday, 5th.—The New York, Colonel Mulford's
"exchange" boat, is alongside the wharf to-day, and
any number of rumors fill the ship, of speedy depart-

ure. These are confirmed somewhat by the arrival of
Mr. Beebee, agent of the Sanitary Commission, with
large supplies for the Yankee prisoners, who will be
received in exchange for us. Some of these supplies
failed to reach Savannah, as the guards broke into the
treasure to-night, and all got gloriously drunk on the
liquid contributions of the Commission.

Sunday, 6th.—A prize steamer loaded with cotton
came in to-day, and two more during the week. These
vessels with their cargoes are sold after condemnation
by a prize court, and half the proceeds turned over to
the government. One-twentieth of the remaining half
goes to the commandant of the North Atlantic squadron, and the rest is divided among the officers and
crew of the capturing vessel. Under this rule, it is
estimated that Porter's share of prize-money, while on
duty here up to this time—about twenty-five days—
will amount to twenty thousand dollars. Last night
we were aroused by an indiscriminate firing throughout the fleet, and on getting on deck, found the harbor
ablaze with colored lights, and guns going off in every
direction—a sham naval battle at night. This, and
the constant drilling at the guns, with the daily practice of launch-drill, indicate an early and vigorous naval
attack in some direction—probably Wilmington; and
as an armada is accumulating here, already more
powerful than any ever set afloat from the days of the
Argonauts, we may look for a powerful blow, when it
is delivered. Boat-loads of soldiers are constantly
passing down the river. These are patriots of the
right political stripe, who are being furloughed to go
home to vote—"no other need apply."

At half-past four on the evening of Tuesday, the 8th, we weighed anchor, and in company with the Atlantic, Baltic, Illinois, Herman Livingstone, and two or three empty transports, we started for Hilton Head, where we arrived about nine o'clock, Thursday night. This, as the world knows, is the *point d'appui* of the military operations of the enemy in South Carolina.

Quite a village has sprung up in the harbor, and about a mile north of this is Mitchell-town, named after the astronomer general, who left his appropriate star-gazing in the Cincinnati Observatory to civilize Southern barbarians. But their country revenged their wrongs, by poisoning his blood, and that of "many a tyrant since," with the deadly malaria of the coast, and so ended that and all other mundane business for the "astronomer-royal" of Porkopolis.

Mitchell-town is quite an interesting locality, as the scene of a grand educational and civilizing experiment on the blacks, whereby the problem of the improvability of that singular race was sought to be solved. How impenetrable the mystery that envelops these slighted members of the great family! For at least forty centuries they have held undisputed possession of a continent, and yet their passing generations have not left a trace on the page of history. Time has overflowed with miracles of human achievement wherever else man's foot has trod, but here there is only a dreary blank. In all these teeming centuries *they* have stood still. They have written no book, painted no picture, carved no statue, built no temple, established no laws, launched no ships, developed no language, achieved no invention. The wisdom of the Egyptians was at their door, and they lit no lamps from that bright torch. The Arab startled Europe with his advances in mathematics and natural science, filling the northern sky of Africa with an aurora of scientific light; but its ray could not penetrate the invincible ignorance of the Ethiopian. Christianity was planted there by martyrs of the apostolic age, and stifled and died in the mephitic air. Civilization, upheld by the concurrent efforts of the most powerful States, succumbed to influences more powerful than arms, treasures, and fanaticism combined, and the African stands now, as did his ancestors in the days of the Pharaohs, a moral and physical mystery in the earth—the victim of some dread judgment of God, powerful, searching, pervasive, and irreversible.

Servus servorum he is to-day, notwithstanding all the appliances of philanthropy and legislation for his improvement. A servant of servants he was when the new world sprang into the knowledge of man. A servant of servants was he when the imperial eagles flashed first over the sands of the British coast. A servant of servants was he when the pyramids were planted on their solid foundations—when the Sphinx first lorded it over the sands of the Nile—when Judah's daughters sat by the rivers of Babylon—when Nineveh the mighty wrought its wondrous history. And thus, as we turn backward to the earliest mementoes of man, we find, even in that elaborate sign-language which antedated letters and was its barbaric prototype, the unmistakable effigy of the negro with

all the physical characteristics which distinguish him
to-day, carved *with a rope around his neck,* to tell
the condition and fate of the predestined *servus ser-*
vorum!

      *   *   *   *   *   *

How did the Mitchell-town experiment succeed?
Sadly I fear. Some prying, and no doubt slanderous
correspondent of a copperhead journal, not having
the fear of Fred Douglas or Salmon Chase (namesake
of the reproach of American judgeship) before his
eyes, declares that several assorted samples of first-class
Yankee school-marms were exported to Mitchell-town,
armed with acres of spelling-books, pinafores, slate-
pencils, and sugar-candy, for the reclaiming of the
unregenerate Pompeys and pickaninnies of South
Carolina; and divers bulbous Sleeks and attenuated
Progrims electrified the world with the wonders—to
come. Monthly reports kept alive the excitement,
and monthly contributions kept alive the reports,
until a half a year having elapsed, it leaked out that
the "marms" had, with singular unanimity, resolved
upon a grand and unusual act of consecration to the
cause, to which the Hindoo "suttee" is not a circumstance. Pursuing their martyr-like resolve to devote
themselves entirely to the elevation of the poor blacks,
they magnanimously determined to waive all paltry
prejudices as to color, and a general amalgamation
ensued, and—and—in short, school-teaching became
soon entirely out of the question. Poor school-marms!
They were incontinently dismissed by the heartless
Government, and the elevation of the unbleached
received a mortal blow. Pitiable indeed was the case

of these Connecticut martyrs, and miserably cruel the conduct of Uncle Sam. Verily, verily, republics *are* ungrateful. Nothing is left to these missionaries of civilization except the reward of a satisfied conscience, and that consolation which springs from the faithful discharge of maternal duties.

We lay in this roadstead until Saturday, when orders came to proceed as near as possible to Fort Pulaski; and in a few hours we were safely moored alongside the single Yankee gunboat which kept watch and ward over the entrance to the Savannah River, and which, by the way, was covered to the tops with a strong netting to prevent enterprising rebels from boarding and capturing her, by one of those "horse marine" movements, which have been among the most amusing and most successful feats of the war.

We remained here all night—a soft, summery night, though late in the fall; and many of us lounged on deck till morning, too much exhilarated by the safe termination of our captivity, and the near approach of home, to waste our hours in the prosaic stupidity of sleep. Major Abrahams, the officer in charge of us, and Lieutenant Gordon, both of the Eighty-fifth Pennsylvania, I met frequently while pacing the deck, and found them quite as anxious to deliver us as we were to be delivered. Their terms of service had expired, and they had been pressed into this service by a piece of military smartness—which is not wisdom either side of the line—in order that some duty might be extorted from them after the legal claim of the Government had expired. Early next morning, the exchange-boat

"New York," with Colonel John E. Mulford, commissioner, aboard, came alongside; we were hurried aboard, and with three rousing cheers for the Northern Light and her officers and crew, steamed up-stream to the truce-ground, some ten miles up the river. Here we were met by a deputation of citizens and a squad of that excellent society of Good Samaritans, who succored the soldiers of both armies on every field and under all circumstances, from the spring of 1862 to the end of the war, the Richmond Ambulance Committee, and transferring ourselves with commendable speed—*for invalids*—to an aboriginal craft composed of a railroad shed mortised into a flat-boat, we were soon puffing at a safe speed to Savannah.

It was near midday when we arrived here, amid the enthusiastic shouts of the people, and the enlivening music of a genuine Southern band, vocal with "Dixie."

How joyfully and well those citizens met us, who, sixty days thereafter, passed such extremely "loyal" resolutions at the bidding of Tecumseh Sherman, it is not pleasant now to dwell upon. Sixty days are an æon in these times.

Our arrival was the signal for a general massacre of all bipeds furnished with feathers, in that vicinage, and the prisoners fared as sumptuously as Dives, however deficient—and the lack therein was miserable—*in fine linen,* or, indeed, linen of any sort.

Savannah is the most beautiful Atlantic city of the South, and we found, in her long, level streets, and her spacious and elegant squares, agreeable means of passing our walking hours. An interview with General McLaws enabled me to obtain passes for my "fellow militia-men" and myself, and the next evening I bade adieu to Georgia. After numberless and most perilous adventures, such as infallibly befall those who go down into the land in railroad cars, I arrived in Petersburg on the night of Thursday—tired, hungry, and unkempt, but profoundly grateful withal to that overruling Providence who had preserved me unharmed amid the perils of Yankee prisons, the raging ocean, and the Piedmont Railroad.

An imperial autumn moon was flooding the earth with a sea of silver sheen, checkering the city with its splendid contrasts of dreamy lights, and bold, deep shadows, as I trod its deserted streets, ploughed in many a quarter with the track of the crushing shell and shot; and the sharp, perpetual ring of the picket's rifle, gave its martial echo to every footfall that pressed the pavement. Every thing suggested strife, contest, and the wreck and desolation of war. I passed the churches, and found that their yards had been converted into burial-grounds—the public cemetery being within reach of the enemy's guns, and therefore, unapproachable. In many private-grounds I noticed embankments with which bomb-proofs were covered, for the safety of the citizens during the frequent bombardments. Many of the lower stories of dwellings were protected by barricades of cotton-bales: on every side, in a word, were monuments at once of the perils and the fortitude of the gallant people, who, through a siege of nine months, during which they have suffered every extremity of war, save famine, and almost that, have nobly, and without the first murmur of complaint, devoted themselves and their all to the cause,—*coveting,* as it were, the honor of civic martyrdom, from which so many others have meanly shrunk. Well and worthily did the noble little town win her title of "Cockade," in 1812; and nobler and more indisputable is her right to the distinction now.

How suggestive was all this! In leaving prison, I found I had not come to peace, but to the presence and the centre of war, and I read in the melancholy but mute lessons of the solemn, silent tombs, that started like unbidden ghosts out of the shadow of each house of worship, the record of mortal dangers, not to men alone, but to inoffensive and helpless women and children. Still, there required no subtle philosophy to find abundant consolation amid all this—was I not, with each step of my hurrying feet, fast approaching, nearer and nearer, to the welcome and the warmth of the lips and hearts and hearth of Home?

Other Civil War titles offered by *Digital Scanning, Inc.*

Debates of Lincoln and Douglas,
by William Schouler
As Published in 1868.
TP: 1582180008 ($14.95)
HC: 1582180083 ($24.95)

McClellan's Own Story,
by George B. McClellan
As Published in 1887.
TP: 1582180075 ($29.95)
HC: 1-582180369 ($44.95)

The Battle of Gettysburg,
by Comte de Paris
As Published in 1886.
TP: 1582180652 ($17.95)
HC: 1582180660 ($29.95)

Daring and Suffering,
by Lt. William Pittenger
As Published in 1863.
TP: 158218075X ($15.95)
HC: 1582180768 ($25.95)

Personal Memoirs of P. H. Sheridan (2 Volume Set),
by P. H. Sheridan
As Published in 1888.
Volume 1:
TP: 1582181020 ($24.95)
HC: 1582181853 ($34.95)
Volume 2:
TP: 1582181039 ($24.95)
HC: 1582181861 ($34.95)

Personal Memoirs of Gen. W. T. Sherman (2 Volume Set),
by P. H. Sheridan
As Published in 1891.
Volume 1:
TP: 1582181047 ($24.95)
HC: 158218187X ($37.95)
Volume 2:
TP: 1582181055 ($24.95)
HC: 1582181888 ($37.95)

Personal Memoirs of U. S. Grant (2 Volume Set)
by U. S. Grant
As Published in 1885.
Volume 1:
TP: 1582181063 ($24.95)
HC: 1582181896 ($39.95)
Volume 2:
TP: 1582181071 ($24.95)
HC: 158218190X ($39.95)

Six Months at the White House,
by F. B. Carpenter
As Published in 1866.
TP: 1582181209 ($19.95)
HC: 1582181233 ($29.95)

The Soldier's Story of His Captivity at Andersonville, Belle Isle, and Other Rebel Prisons,
by Warren Lee Goss
As Published in 1866.
TP: 1582182272 ($19.95)
HC: 1582182280 ($34.95)

The Life of Abraham Lincoln (4 Volume series combined into 2 Volumes),
by Ida Tarbell
As Published in 1900.
Volumes 1 & 2:
TP: 1582181241 ($24.95)
HC: 1582181837 ($37.95)
Volumes 3 & 4:
TP: 158218125X ($24.95)
HC: 1582181845 ($37.95)

The History of the Andrews Railroad Raid,
by William Pittenger
As Published in 1887.
TP: 1582181926 ($24.95)
HC: 1582181918 ($34.95)

Deeds of Daring,
by D.M. Kelsey
As Published in 1898.
TP: 1582181543 ($29.95)
HC: 1582181551 ($39.95)

Nurse and Spy in the Union Army,
by Emma Edmonds
As Published in 1865.
TP: 1582181586 ($19.95)
HC: 1582181594 ($29.95)

The Life of Stonewall Jackson,
by John Esten Cooke
originally published
by Charles B. Richardson
As Published in 1863.
TP: 1582182515 ($15.95)
HC: 1582182523 ($29.95)

Capturing a Locomotive,
by William Pittenger
As Published in 1885.
TP: 1582182159 ($19.95)
HC: 1582182167 ($29.95)

Reminiscences of Forts Sumter and Moultrie,
by Abner Doubleday
As Published in 1876.
TP: 1582182795 ($11.95)
HC: 1582182809 ($24.95)

Herndon's Lincoln: The True Story of a Great Life,
by William H. Herndon
As Published in 1888.
TP: 158218108X ($29.95)
HC: 1582181365 ($39.95)

Genesis of the Civil War: The Story of Sumter,
by Samuel Wylie Crawford
As Published in 1887.
TP: 1582181128 ($24.95)
HC: 1582181381 ($34.95)

**The True Story
of Andersonville Prison,**
*by James Madison Page
and M.J. Haley*
As Published in 1908.
TP: 1582181462 ($14.95)
HC: 1582181470 ($24.95)

The Battle of Gettysburg,
by Samuel A. Drake
As Published in 1892.
TP: 1582183260 ($9.95)
HC: 1582183279 ($24.95)

**The Prison Life of
Jefferson Davis,**
by John L. Craven
As Published in 1866.
TP: 1582185107 ($19.95)
HC: 1582185115 ($34.95)

**John Brown and His Men
(2 Volume Set),**
by Richard Hinton
As Published in 1894.
Volume 1:
TP: 1582182949 ($19.95)
HC: 1582182957 ($32.95)
Volumes 2:
TP: 1582183562 ($19.95)
HC: 1582183600 ($32.95)

**Stonewall Jackson,
The Life and Military
Career of Thomas
Jonathan Jackson,**
by Markinfield Addey
As Published in 1863.
TP: 1582183503 ($12.95)
HC: 1582183511 ($25.95)

**Life and Campainings
of Lt. Gen. Thomas J.
Jackson,**
by Robert Lewis Dabney
As Published in 1866.
TP: 1582186367 ($34.95)
HC: 1582186375 ($45.95)

Lee's Sharpshooters,
by Major W. S. Dunlop
As Published in 1889.
TP: 158218612X ($24.95)
HC: 1582186138 ($37.95)

Tenting on the Plains,
by Elizabeth Custer
As Published in 1887.
TP: 1582180504 ($29.95)
HC: 1582180512 ($39.95)

**The Cruise of the Alabama
and The Sumter,**
by Ralph Semmes
As Published in 1864.
TP: 1582183546 ($17.95)
HC: 1582183554 ($31.95)

**Army Life in a
Black Regiment,**
by Thomas Wentworth Higgins
As Published in 1870.
TP: 1582183589 ($15.95)
HC: 1582183597 ($29.95)

**Reminiscences of
Winfield Scott Hancock,**
by A. R. Hancock
As Published in 1887.
TP: 1582180555 ($19.95)
HC: 1582180563 ($29.95)

**Southern Generals
Who They Are,
And What They Have Done**
by Charles B. Richardson
As Published in 1865.
TP: 1582182213 ($24.95)
HC: 1582182221 ($39.95)

To order any of the titles listed:

*Contact your local bookstore and order through *Ingram Books.*
*Contact the publisher directly
  (for general information or special event purchases):
    Digital Scanning, Inc.
    344 Gannett Rd., Scituate, MA 02066
    Phone: (781) 545-2100 Fax: (781) 545-4908 Toll Free in the U.S.: 888-349-444
    email: books@digitalscanning.com
    www.digitalscanning.com

www.ingramcontent.com/pod-product-compliance
Lightning Source LLC
Chambersburg PA
CBHW030529100426
42813CB00001B/193